Role Models

Examples of Character & Leadership

Joseph M. Hoedel, Ph.D.

Role Models: Examples of Character & Leadership

Publisher:
Character Development Group, Inc.
366 Bella Vista Dr.
Boone, NC 28607
888.262.0572
E-mail: Info@CharacterEducation.com
www.CharacterEducation.com

Layout by Sara Sanders, SHS Design

ISBN-10: 1-892056-42-9
ISBN-13: 978-1-892056-42-9

Printed in the United States of America

Dedication

To our daughter, Hope:
May your mother and I possess the wisdom and integrity to provide you with a solid foundation of character to help you become a leader of tomorrow. I hope we can live up to the high standards set by our parents, thereby making us worthy of the grandest of all titles—your role model.

COVER PHOTO ACKNOWLEDGMENTS

Contents

Preface

Wanted: Positive Role Models

Tiger Woods defines a role model as someone who embraces the responsibility of influencing others positively. It's really that simple—anyone can be a role model. We are all in a position to positively influence other human beings. Each one of us has been in numerous situations where we were faced with choices: either offer help to someone in need or turn the other way; either be critical or say something positive; either take the easy way out or do the right thing. Taking on the responsibility of being a role model does not require you to shoot hoops, break a world record, or act in a movie. You don't even have to be rich or famous. In fact, the best role models are regular people who come directly from the local community. They do the little things that make a big difference. They volunteer to mentor a young person, donate to a favorite charity, or lend a helping hand to a friend. The question is, will you embrace this responsibility or shrug it off as a task for someone else? If we live under the assumption that acting as a role model is always someone else's responsibility, what kind of world would we live in? Whether we like it or not, if we want people to treat us with respect, we need to be respectful of others. If we want our neighbors to be helpful to us, we need to be helpful to our neighbors. Even if these acts of kindness go unnoticed, they are a strong testament to good character.

Unfortunately, it seems that role models fail us every day. Pick up any newspaper or watch the nightly news and you will see someone caught up in an ugly scandal. Athletes are involved in point-shaving scandals, take money from boosters, or use performance-enhancing drugs to unfairly advance their careers. Married politicians admit to having affairs and taking bribes. Corporate executives act so unethically that they are bankrupting once-powerful companies and leaving loyal employees literally penniless. Hollywood actors and other pop culture figures are routinely convicted of drug possession or domestic violence.

Everyone makes mistakes, but the frequency and severity of these lapses in character are alarming. For two years I asked my high school students to bring in examples of lapses in character. Each week the students would cut out articles from papers and assorted magazines or bring in video clips from *ESPN Sports Center, Entertainment Tonight,* or other nightly news shows. Not once did a student fail to bring in news of a well-known person exhibiting a lack of good character.

The following are some notable examples of the unfortunate trend we see every day in America. In a well-documented case, members of the Duke Lacrosse team hired two strippers to provide "entertainment" at an off-campus party. One of these strippers claimed to have been raped by three members of the team. Mike Pressler, the men's head lacrosse coach resigned in disgrace and the university president cancelled the season. Despite inconsistencies in the alleged victim's story and any DNA evidence to support her accusations, Durham County District Attorney, Mike Nifrong, took the case on with a vengeance. He made inflammatory remarks about the three defendants and essentially convicted them in the media. There was just one problem with this rush to judgment—the players were innocent. In 2007, Mike Nifrong was disbarred for breaking more than two dozen rules of professional conduct and resigned as the district attorney. It appears that there are ethical lessons to be learned by everyone in this case.

Paris Hilton was arrested for driving under the influence in 2006. She was sentenced to three years probation. She twice broke the terms of her probation by driving without a license. After showing up late for her own hearing, Judge Michael Sauer sentenced her to 45 days in jail. She was literally crying and calling for her mother as she was hauled off to jail. At least in this case, her celebrity status did not put her above the law. In a recent baseball scandal, it was reported that up to 10% of professional players use steroids. Because drug tests are anonymous, the public doesn't know who is guilty. But recent home run records will forever be tainted in the minds of many baseball fans. And in a 2004 scandal with global consequences, U.S. soldiers in Iraq violated the Geneva Convention by humiliating and abusing prisoners of war, even taking photographs of their actions. Unfortunately, the acts of a few individuals cast a negative shadow on every soldier proudly serving in the military.

Sadly, the list could go on and on. I believe that this immoral behavior lowers the bar for our youth. In most cases, Americans do not shun these individuals or put them in a social time-out. With so many star athletes, for example, continuing to receive attention and accolades in spite of embarrassing scandals, high school student-athletes do not have much incentive to walk the straight and narrow.

These so-called role models are sending the wrong message to young people. But perhaps they should not even be labeled as role models. Maybe Charles Barkley had it right. In a 1993 Nike commercial, he claimed that he should not be considered a role model simply because he could put a basketball through a hoop. Instead, he said, parents and teachers are the true role models. If we agree with Barkley, we should all turn our collective attention to people who consistently do the right thing. However, the media sensationalize negative stories and often ignore or gloss over stories of people who are meeting societal expectations—that is, those who treat others with respect, are honest in their actions and words, and take personal responsibility for their mistakes. For some reason those stories don't have a lot of pizzazz or oomph. The end result is that young people don't identify with examples of people who display good character. How unfortunate!

As Americans, we have always known the importance of character. Our country was founded on concepts such as discipline, integrity, perseverance, responsibility, and respect.

George Washington once said, "I hope that I shall always possess firmness and virtue enough to maintain what I consider the best of all titles—the character of an honest person." Another famous president, Theodore Roosevelt, wrote, "To educate a person in mind and not morals is to educate a menace to society." In the last half of the 20th century, Martin Luther King Jr. spoke about the importance of character when he said, "We must remember that intelligence is not enough. Intelligence plus character—that is the goal of true education."

We do not focus on these important virtues as much as we should. When a neighbor treats his wife with compassion, spends quality time with his kids, and puts in a full day of work each day, he is not recognized for displaying good character. However, if he cheats on his wife, abuses his children, or steals from the company, he will be the talk of the town. Maybe this is a good sign—should we really praise people for doing the right thing? It is encouraging that we are still appalled by scandal and controversy. However, we need to focus on educating young people about the character traits that will help them to become responsible adults who contribute to the good of society.

My reason for writing this book is to draw attention to people who demonstrate positive character traits every day. We need to read about these true role models and raise our expectations of humanity. To illustrate the importance of good character, I chose to highlight seventeen Americans who exemplify a particular positive character trait. I limited the book to Americans only because I consider myself a patriot, and I strongly believe in the principles our country was founded on. I researched many individuals before finally settling on those highlighted here. Some are contemporary figures we can look to every day. Others have been dead for many years, but they deserve our long-lasting respect and gratitude. Regardless of when these individuals were born or what profession they chose, we should study their lives, applaud them, and strive to emulate them.

It should not be surprising to learn that the people highlighted in this book typically demonstrated more than one positive character trait. For example, Oprah Winfrey was selected for the compassion she has for other people, and yet she has also demonstrated perseverance in overcoming significant obstacles to achieve the success she enjoys today. Tiger Woods was selected because he exhibited commitment and dedication in his intense preparation to become the world's best golfer. At the same time, he has impeccable integrity. As such, these individuals are worthy of being called "role models."

I hope that you, the reader, are inspired to be more like the seventeen individuals profiled in this book. If so, the world will undoubtedly be a better place. I also hope this book inspires you to research and emulate other strong role models, including those in your own community. Thank them for their attitude and behavior. One definition of character is "doing what's right, even when no one is looking." That may be so, but if you are looking and observe a friend or a neighbor demonstrating outstanding character, be sure to commend that person and let them know that they deserve to be called a role model. Each person doing his or her small part will make our world a better place for current and future generations.

Mattie Stepanek

Attitude

In many ways, Mattie Stepanek was an ordinary kid. The skinny thirteen-year-old with blue eyes and blond hair liked pizza, barbequed ribs, and chocolate ice cream. He loved watching Saturday morning cartoons and enjoyed playing video games. Mattie's favorite athletic teams were the Baltimore Orioles and the Washington Redskins. He wasn't fond of cleaning his room and would sometimes procrastinate on his homework. The most striking feature about Mattie was his smile. If you didn't know any better, you would think this happy-go-lucky child had it easy.

However, several noticeable characteristics set him apart from other kids his age. Mattie was confined to a wheelchair to help him move from place to place. He also had a tube that stuck out of the front of his neck called a tracheotomy, which in addition to a ventilator and oxygen tanks, helped him breathe. These extra devices were necessary because Mattie suffered from a rare form of muscular dystrophy. Unfortunately, this disease kept Mattie in and out of hospitals for most of his abbreviated life. He required weekly blood transfusions and was hooked up to an IV each night to stabilize his blood pressure. At several points in Mattie's short life, his doctors were convinced he would not survive. His mother commented, "Mattie moves back and forth between probably dying and possibly dying." Life never treated Mattie fairly.

However, this little boy never asked for life to be fair or easy. Despite the obstacles that life threw at him, Mattie approached every day with a positive attitude. He might not have been able to control all facets of his life, but he knew that "attitude is a choice," and he continually chose to be an optimist. He was an extraordinary person with a kind heart. "With his unabashed enthusiasm for life, Mattie has charmed everyone who has crossed his path," Jim Hawkins of Children's Hospice International said. "Little Mattie has somehow acquired more wisdom in his short life than most of us do after decades of living." Sadly, Mattie's life was cut short on June 22, 2004, when he died at the age of thirteen from complications related to muscular dystrophy.

Mattie Stepanek is the youngest person profiled in this book. His life clearly demonstrates that good character is not just reserved for adults. In fact, character knows no boundaries when it comes to age, ethnic background, gender, or religion. Every person is capable of taking responsibility for themselves, treating others with respect and acting with integrity. Doing so, however, requires a conscious choice. Every day of his life, Mattie strived to be a better person and to make a positive difference in the lives of others. Former President Jimmy Carter said, "Even a child who lives ten or eleven years can have an enormous impact, and I think Mattie is one of those special people." Millions of Americans have lived longer lives, but few inspired more people than Mattie did. While most adolescents can't wait to reach adulthood, Mattie made his mark at a young age by living each and every day to the fullest, despite overwhelming obstacles.

Mattie was born on July 17, 1990, in Washington, D.C. He was born into a large family that included two older brothers and a younger sister. However, muscular dystrophy wreaked havoc on his family over a short period of time. Mattie's oldest brother died from the disease at the age of two, and his older sister had died before Mattie was born, when she was just six months old. At first, doctors could not conclusively identify the cause of these premature deaths. However, in 1992 Mattie's mother was diagnosed with adult-onset muscular dystrophy. The disease is genetic and unfortunately, she had passed it on to her children. Still grief-stricken from the death of her two oldest children, she learned that her third child, Jamie, and her youngest child, Mattie, also suffered from this debilitating disease. In what was turning out to be the cruelest of all fates, Jamie died at the age of four. At the time of Jamie's death, Mattie was only three. The mind of a three-year-old has trouble understanding the concept of death. Mattie remembered the first time he saw his older brother in his small white casket. "I thought the funeral was a party for him, that he was playing hide-and-seek with me. I kept saying, 'You can come out now, Jamie.'" The permanency of Jamie's death finally hit Mattie when they placed his brother's casket in the ground.

Mattie's feelings were overwhelming and intense. To cope with the loss of his beloved brother, he began telling his mother what was in his heart. "Shh! Listen! That's my heartsong!" he often said. Mattie's mom thought his words were poetic and began writing them down. Years later she said, "I thought it was sweet at the time. Nothing more than sweet." The words poured out of Mattie and he began to feel better. Through writing about his emotions, he began to find inner peace. He called these poems "heartsongs." He explained what he meant by the unusual term: "A heartsong is like your inner message. It's your inner beauty."

As Mattie's life progressed, he had more sad events to write about, including his parents' divorce. Not only had he lost three of his siblings, but he was losing the solid foundation of a two-parent household. After the divorce, Mattie and his mother moved into a small apartment. Loss was becoming a major theme in Mattie's life, and he continued to express his emotions through his poetry. By the time he was six, Mattie had written hundreds of poems. The poems continued to help him deal with the difficult realities of his life. Yet he didn't just write about his sorrow. He wrote about his hopes and dreams. Despite all the heartache in his life, he was filled with undying optimism. His mother astutely noted, "In spite of the pain and in spite of the times that he says 'why me?' he is an eternal optimist."

Mattie had a unique gift for looking at the bright side of things. "The disease is a curse at first sight, but I wouldn't be me without it," he said. "I haven't given up. I don't sit in the corner and cry about my life. I thank God for life. I make the fullest of it." Thanks largely to this positive attitude, he accomplished more than anyone thought possible. Mattie was extremely intelligent and skipped several grades in elementary school. Unfortunately, his illness caused him to miss so much school that his mother decided to begin home schooling him when he was nine. Mattie explained, "Even though I would have some good days, I missed so much school that it was like I wasn't really a part of the class anymore." In the one-on-one environment that home schooling provides, Mattie zoomed through middle school. His mother had a master's degree in education, so she introduced her son to a curriculum that included a healthy mix of high school and college courses. Much of his time was spent reading classic literature, studying history, and suffering through algebra.

Mattie seemed to want to fit as much into his short life as he could. One of the areas in which he excelled was martial arts. Before he was confined to a wheelchair, Mattie earned a black belt in Hapkido. Quite a remarkable feat for a small child, but as Mattie put it, "I choose to live until death, not spend the time dying until death occurs." When the muscles in his legs weakened to the point that he had to use a wheelchair, he took the news in stride and actually nicknamed the chair "Slick." "It's disappointing that I haven't been able to rollerblade and skateboard, but you know what? I've still had the best time," Mattie said. "And because of my attitude, I've had a blast in the wheelchair."

The specific name of Mattie's illness is *dysautonomic mitochondrial myopathy*, one of the forty-three neuromuscular diseases for which the Muscular Dystrophy Association (MDA) seeks a cure. Mattie's disease is a rare form of muscular dystrophy that impairs the heart rate, breathing, blood pressure, and digestion. It also gradually weakens a person's muscles, limiting the normal movement of arms and legs. The disease is particularly cruel because it gradually steals a person's abilities, leaving them powerless to do anything to stop it. For some reason, patients who are afflicted with the disease at an early age have a much shorter life expectancy than those who are diagnosed as adults. Mattie wasn't expected to live much longer than his siblings, but he kept beating the odds. "Every year the doctors tell my mom that I won't make it another year—yet here I am," he said.

The pain associated with muscular dystrophy can be excruciating. "The other day I felt like somebody was banging a hammer into my spine," Mattie said. On one occasion, blood began to seep out of his lips, fingers, and toes. One of the worst bouts he had with the disease occurred during the summer of 2001. While in the intensive care unit, Mattie slipped into a coma for approximately two weeks. Even though he eventually woke up, his trachea flooded with water, making it nearly impossible for Mattie to breathe. The situation was grim; doctors told his mother that he had less than three days to live. It was about this time that the Make-A-Wish Foundation got involved.

The foundation grants final wishes to terminally ill children all over the world. Mattie's wish was to meet his hero, former President Jimmy Carter. Mattie admired President Carter because of his efforts to inspire peace all over the world. President Carter surprised Mattie with a visit to his hospital room. According to Mattie's mother, it was the first and only time in his life that he was speechless. President Carter said they formed an "instantaneous bond of love." He went on to say, "That meeting and our subsequent relationship has literally changed my life for the better." The visit must have had an equally positive impact on Mattie's spirit because he miraculously recovered and went home. Apparently, Mattie still had work to do.

His other two wishes were to get the hundreds of poems he had written published and to appear on *The Oprah Winfrey Show*. He began with his mission to publish a book of his poetry. He and his mother sent his poems to dozens of publishers, but no one expressed interest. Mattie remained optimistic and determined. Finally, a small company, VSP Publishers, said yes and agreed to print a slim volume of his poems in a book entitled *Heartsongs*. Peter Barnes, a VSP representative, described his reaction upon reading Mattie's poetry for the first time. "I was stunned. It was perceptive and thoughtful." The company didn't expect a large response to the book, so they printed only 200 copies. VSP Publishers likely hypothesized that printing the book was a good public relations move and the small number of books could be given to Mattie's close friends and family.

However, once Mattie began promoting his book the response was enthusiastic and overwhelming. Audiences were inspired by listening to a ten-year-old with such a debilitating disease talk so optimistically about life, love, and peace. His message gave people hope and encouraged them to believe in the power of goodness. Jerry Lewis, chairperson of MDA, said, "His example made people want to reach for the best within themselves." When Oprah Winfrey heard about Mattie's remarkable story, she chartered a private jet to escort him to Chicago for an appearance on her show. "I fell in love with him," Oprah said. She was inspired by his words and his positive attitude. They continued their relationship via e-mail. She later said of Mattie, "There was no braver soul, nor bigger spirit in so small and frail a body."

Mattie continued to promote his book of poetry on talk shows and news programs around the country. The book quickly climbed to the top of the *New York Times* bestseller list, selling more than 500,000 copies. Clearly, Mattie's poems struck a chord with Americans. Before long, there was a demand for more of his poetry. People wanted to view the beauty of the world through his eyes. Mattie went on to publish four more books, all of which contained the heartsongs theme: *Journey Through Heartsongs, Hope Through Heartsongs, Celebrate Through Heartsongs* and *Loving Through Heartsongs*. All of the books became bestsellers and together sold more than two million copies. As a tribute to his exceptional work, the Library of Congress requested a bound anthology of his works to be placed in the national archives.

By the age of eleven, all three of Mattie's wishes had been

fulfilled. He had talked about world peace with President Carter, appeared on *The Oprah Winfrey Show*, and published his poetry to a wide audience. Most people his age would have been more than satisfied with these impressive achievements, but Mattie set additional goals. His optimism was clear when he wrote a list detailing his long-term goals of getting married, becoming a father, and living to be 101. "I have big dreams and I don't stop dreaming them until they happen," he wrote in an e-mail message to Oprah. Mattie loved making lists and setting goals—it kept him going. Mattie didn't understand how some able-bodied people went through life without dreams, goals, and ambitions.

While Mattie died before he was able to achieve his long-term goals, he expressed a powerful philosophy that remains with us today. "Remember to play after every storm." It's a reminder that we all need to celebrate our accomplishments, even when life continues to knock us down. Mattie wanted to be remembered as "a poet, a philosopher who plays, and a peacemaker." He expanded on this altruistic mission by saying, "We have to make peace an attitude. Then we have to make it a habit. Finally, we must decide to live peace, to share it around the world—not just talk about it." One of Mattie's unrealized goals was to write a book with President Carter, who had just won the 2002 Nobel Peace Prize. Mattie even had an appropriate title picked out—*Just Peace.*

From 2002–2004 Mattie served as the MDA National Ambassador and helped to raise money to find a cure for muscular dystrophy. When asked about his role with the organization, he was always upbeat. "I love doing stuff for MDA and am glad that I can continue to help," he said. "We're raising money for a cure and on the way we're finding ways to keep celebrating." While appearing on the annual Labor Day telethon, Mattie became fast friends with Jerry Lewis. Lewis is so closely associated with MDA that kids diagnosed with the disease are often referred to as "Jerry's Kids." Lewis was particularly taken in by Mattie's charisma, saying, "With Mattie, there was always a silver lining. Life threw its worst at him and he

Muscular Dystrophy Association National Goodwill Ambassador Mattie Stepanek and National Chairman Jerry Lewis.
Photo courtesy of the Muscular Dystrophy Association.

responded by seeing the good. He was—he is—a shining star."

This child who was not supposed to live more than a few years in this world was living out his dreams. And the only thing he asked for was time—time to spread his message of peace.

If you ask most little boys what they want for Christmas, they almost always recite a long list of toys. When Oprah asked Mattie what he wanted for Christmas, he humbly said, "If it's not too much trouble, I'd like you to pray for me." When his mother was asked what she wished for, she said, "I want time with my son. I want time that we both have to continue celebrating life." Their simple wishes remind us just how precious life really is. If we could just take a step back and view life from Mattie's perspective, we would soon realize how insignificant our daily problems can be. Mattie's example should teach us not to be so concerned with the minor details of life.

Mattie could sense his time was running short. In an e-mail message to Oprah near the end of his life, he wrote, "My body is trying to die more and more each year, even though my spirit is trying to keep it going even just a little bit longer." Mattie spent much of his life in and out of hospitals, and as he got older the complications from the disease became more severe.

His heart actually stopped beating for forty-five minutes early in 2004, before he was finally revived by doctors. In March of that year, Mattie checked into the hospital for the last time. He was in unbearable pain. It was nearly impossible for him to breathe, and his doctors couldn't expand his lungs any more. According to his mother, he indicated that he was ready to die, but kept asking her if he had done enough. With tears in her eyes, she said, "You are everything God created people to be. You have done everything you came here for. I'll be okay. I love you." She was giving her son permission to die. She continued to hold him and kiss him. She said she wanted to give him enough kisses for eternity. A few moments later, Mattie passed away in his mother's arms.

During his lifetime, Mattie inspired thousands of people and made many friends. An estimated 1,300 people attended his funeral. Close friends and complete strangers alike came to pay their final respects. His two special friends, President Jimmy Carter and Oprah Winfrey, gave moving eulogies. President Carter said, "We [my wife and I] have known kings and queens, and we've known presidents and prime ministers, but the most extraordinary person whom I have ever known in my life is Mattie Stepanek." This was high praise coming from a seventy-nine-year-old former president and Nobel Peace Prize winner. Oprah was equally impressed with this young man's spirit. "I could not believe so much wisdom, so much power, so much grace, so much strength and love could come from one ten-year-old little boy," she said. Near the end of her eulogy, Oprah added, "I know that his heartsong has left a heart print in my life. A heart print that abides with me even now."

Through his work with MDA, Mattie had created a special relationship with firefighters. In accordance with his wishes, Mattie's casket was carried to the cemetery in a bright red fire truck. Over 1,000 fire fighters lined the streets as a special tribute to this little boy with a big heart. He was buried as a fallen firefighter, a rare honor for a child. His name was also added to the Fallen Fire Fighter Wall of Honor. As his body was carried to the cemetery, one of the last images seen by Mattie's friends and family was a sticker on his casket that read: "Be a peacemaker."

Mattie Stepanek was one of a kind, no question about it. He packed a lifetime of living into his thirteen years. However, there is a piece of him in every one of us. It's all about attitude! Don't take life for granted. No one is promised tomorrow, but a positive attitude can change the outcome of today. Each of us has the power to change the way we approach school, work, and family. Instead of complaining about trivial problems, we should spend our time celebrating our accomplishments. Be thankful for what life has given you each and every day. Choose to look for the beauty in all situations and live each day to the fullest. Imagine what this world would be like if we all strived to approach life with Mattie's optimism and positive attitude.

Eldrick "Tiger" Woods

Preparation

At the age of two, Tiger Woods was already a celebrity. He was still in diapers when he appeared on *The Mike Douglas Show*—the 1970s version of *The Tonight Show with Jay Leno*—yet he was able to demonstrate a beautiful, rhythmic golf swing. The audience was amazed. Even Bob Hope, another guest on the show and an avid golfer himself, was impressed with Tiger's amazing talent. This was not the first time Tiger Woods had appeared on television and it certainly wouldn't be his last. When he was only five, he appeared on the hit show *That's Incredible.* By the age of thirteen he had appeared on the *Today Show, Good Morning America*, the ESPN network, and countless local programs. In one television interview, when he was just three, Tiger was asked how he had become such a good golfer at such a young age. His response was "Pwactice." He was so young that he had trouble pronouncing the word correctly, but the reporter understood. He then asked Tiger, "How much do you practice?" "About a whole bunch," Tiger replied.

Tiger Woods has always been a phenom in the truest sense of the word. By the time he was twenty, he had won every major amateur tournament and earned every conceivable All-American award. The most prestigious award for a non-professional golfer is the U.S. Amateur. For golfers under the age of fifteen, it is known as the Optimist Internal Junior World. For golfers under the age of eighteen, it is known as the U.S. Junior Amateur. To make it competitive, junior tournaments have age brackets. The best golfers from all over the world play in this tournament. With the exception of only two years, Tiger won this tournament every year from the time he was eight years old until he was twenty. He also received the prestigious Dial Award, which is given to the top national high school male athlete. *Golf Digest* ranked him the number one junior in the country for three straight years.

Most experts regard Tiger Woods as the best junior and arguably the best amateur golfer of all time. Tiger turned pro in 1996, at the age of twenty. It is too early to call him the greatest golfer of all time, but he is well on his way to earning that distinction. What is significant about Tiger Woods, however, is not the number of tournaments he has won, the awards he has received, or the fame that he has earned. Instead, it is important to take a close look at the character traits that went into making him the competitor, champion, and person that he is. What has he done to prepare himself to become so successful? What has he had to overcome? How has he changed the game of golf? What has he given back to the people who idolize and adore him? What kind of character does Tiger Woods have?

To understand him, we must start at the beginning. Many people don't know that his first name is actually Eldrick—a name his mother came up with because it begins with the first letter of his father's name (Earl) and ends with the first letter of her name (Kultida). Soon after Eldrick was born, his father sensed there was something special about him and wanted to give him a unique name. Earl Woods was a retired lieutenant colonel and former member of an elite fighting unit in the U.S. Army. While serving his country during the Vietnam War, Earl fought with and formed a friendship with a member of the South Vietnamese Army. This man saved Earl's life on two separate occasions—once from a sniper's bullet and another time from a bamboo viper. Earl said of his friend, "He was a tiger in combat, so I began calling him Tiger." To honor his friend, Earl nicknamed his son Tiger. To Earl, it seemed like a fitting tribute to the man who had saved his life, and it was a tangible sign that his son was destined for greatness.

Earl Woods first played golf at the age of forty-two and took an immediate liking to the game. As an African American, he believed that the reason blacks were virtually non-existent on the PGA tour was that they were not introduced to golf until later in life, if at all. Instead, most black athletes chose to play basketball, football, or baseball in their youth. Earl was determined to introduce his own son to the game of golf at an early age. He created a practice range in the family's garage by using a piece of carpet and a net to catch the balls. He would practice for hours. When Tiger was just six months old, his father first brought him into the garage to watch. After months of intense observation, Tiger picked up a club that was made especially for him and placed a ball on the carpet. Without any prompting, this nine-month-old infant executed a perfect carbon copy of his father's swing. In describing the moment, Earl said, "I was flabbergasted. I almost fell out of my chair." He ran into the house and shouted to Kultida, "We have a genius on our hands!"

Tiger and the game of golf had been formally introduced. While other toddlers were learning to walk, Tiger was already playing golf. When he was eighteen months old, he played his first hole of golf. Tiger's father was further convinced that his son was destined for great things when, at the age of two, he won the ten-and-under division at a local tournament. People often assume that Tiger's parents forced him to play golf and burdened him with high expectations at an early age. Nothing could be further from the truth. Earl did introduce his son to the game at an unusually young age, but Tiger later explained, "He never pushed me to play. Whether I practiced or played was always my idea." To his credit, Tiger always had a burning desire to improve his performance. Tiger's first golf instructor said, "He had an absolute thirst for it. Every lesson we had, he wanted to learn a brand-new shot." Another swing coach who helped him later in his career had the same assessment. "He is the best student I ever had. He is like a sponge—he soaks up information, and he always wants to learn and get better."

Education was always a top priority at the Woods house. Tiger's mother made him complete his homework before he was permitted to play golf. She also had the ultimate form of discipline at her disposal. "When I need to discipline Tiger," she said at the time, "I take his golf clubs away." Tiger's parents were more concerned that he develop into a great person rather than a great golfer. Earl once said, "If he wants to be a fireman in Umpity-Ump, Tennessee, that's fine as long as he's an upright citizen."

As long as Tiger chose to play golf, his parents demanded two things of him. Number one, he was required to be a good sport. When Tiger was six, he played eighteen holes with a club pro. As improbable as it might seem, Tiger was beating him on the front nine, but eventually lost the friendly match. Tiger left the course in tears and refused to shake the man's hand. His mother told him firmly, "You must be a sportsman, win or lose." Earl and Kultida used golf as a vehicle for teaching their son integrity, responsibility, honesty, and patience. Golf is the only sport that requires a player to call a penalty on himself for breaking the rules. Tiger follows this rule and also always demonstrates good etiquette by honoring golf's gentlemanly traditions. Whenever finishing a round of golf, he removes his hat and shakes the hand of his playing partners.

The other essential requirement specified by Tiger's parents was that he must give his best effort whenever he was playing in a tournament. They made sure he knew that it was okay to lose as long as he gave it his all. According to his father, Tiger mentally quit on the golf course only once. This happened as he blew a big lead in the Orange Bowl Junior Classic. "I could see it in his body language. He didn't want to be there anymore," Earl said. "I pulled him into an empty room and really let him have it. Who do you think you are? How dare you not try your best? You embarrassed yourself and you shamed me." That scolding from his father made a lasting impression on Tiger. Even now, if you listen to Tiger's commentary after a tough day, he often talks about how he was "grinding" it out and scrambling to get the job done. He has a strong commitment to putting forth his best effort in every game. In fact, during one stretch, Tiger did not miss a cut (scoring low enough in the first two days of a tournament to be allowed to play in the final two days) on the PGA Tour in 142 straight tournaments, breaking the record of Byron Nelson, who once played in 113 tournaments without missing a cut in the 1940s.

Tiger's parents laid a foundation for him to be successful. Earl estimates that they spent as much as $20,000 per year supporting Tiger's drive to become the best in the sport. They orchestrated his travels to frequent tournaments around the country and supported him from the sidelines. From a very early age, Tiger had a coach to help him improve. At thirteen, he was probably the youngest person ever to hire a sports psychologist. These professionals were crucial components to "Team Tiger." In some ways, it may appear that Tiger Woods had life handed to him on a silver platter or that his success is due entirely to the talent that he was born with. Neither of these assumptions is true.

To become the best at anything requires more than talent—it requires hard work, discipline, and determination. Tiger had all of these traits and more. The young golfer always had a strong desire to get better and a willingness to overcome any obstacles he encountered. Tiger prepared each and every day for his success. He would often have his mother drop him off at the golf course at dawn and pick him up at dusk. He would deliberately go out and play golf when it rained. When his friends inquired about this seemingly crazy behavior, Tiger would say that he was preparing to win the British Open some day, since it is so often played in adverse weather conditions. In 2000 and 2005, Tiger did win the British Open. Not only did he win the tournament, he broke the record for the lowest total score of all time. His years of careful preparation paid off handsomely.

When Tiger turned six, he began listening to audiotapes with subliminal messages to help develop his mental approach to the game. When listening to the tapes, he could only hear soft music, but embedded in the music were the following phrases: "I will my own destiny. I believe in me. I smile at obstacles. I focus and give it my all." He listened to the tapes so often that he wore them out. To further toughen Tiger's psyche, Earl would intentionally disrupt Tiger's concentration with

Tiger Woods and members of the 1997 Ryder Cup Team pose for a photograph with President Bill Clinton. Photo courtesy of William J. Clinton Presidential Library [P56376-16].

psychological tactics. During Tiger's back swing, for instance, Earl might jingle the change in his pocket, cough loudly, or yell, "Fore," which is the term used in golf to warn people of a ball headed in their direction. Finally, after years of this behavior, Earl stopped using these tactics. He proudly told his son, "You'll never play another who's mentally stronger than you are."

While many teenagers try to figure out ways to avoid physical activity, Tiger was actively seeking ways to exercise. He found a recommended workout regimen in *Golf Digest* that would prepare his body for the game of golf, and he followed it to the letter. Even today he runs and works with weights on a regular basis to ensure that he will never tire in a grueling match.

When Tiger turned thirteen, his golf coach provided the Woods family with the following assessment of Tiger's game: "He can compete on the PGA tour right now. He can do anything the game requires." Before Tiger ever set foot in high school, he received a recruiting letter from the head golf coach at Stanford University. Tiger responded to the coach with his own polite and respectful letter, part of which read, "Thank you for your recent letter expressing Stanford's interest in me as a future student and golfer. I became interested in Stanford's academics while watching the Olympics and Debbie Thomas. My goal is to obtain a quality business education. Your guidelines will be most helpful in preparing me for college life. My GPA this year is 3.86 and I plan to keep it there or higher when I enter high school." Later that year, Tiger admitted that he was ninety percent confident that he would attend Stanford University. In spite of his talent and enormous potential, he was wise enough to know that attending college would provide him with a back-up plan in case he did not make it as a professional golfer.

Six years later, he did enroll at Stanford, where his work ethic at the practice range became legendary. "He was serious at practice," said Stanford teammate Jake Poe. Immediately to the left of the practice range was a dormitory. All the players joked about aiming at the building, knowing that if they hit the shot properly they could curve the flight of the ball with a "slice" swing. But most of them thought better of it, knowing their shots would probably hit the building. Not so with Tiger. He would throw down a ball and aim right at the dormitory. Each time, the ball miraculously turned back toward the driving range. His teammates watched in awe. "He hit shots I'd never seen before," Poe said. "It got to the point where nothing surprised me about his game."

While a student-athlete at Stanford, Tiger won every championship and honor imaginable. He won the Pacific 10 Conference Championship by fourteen strokes, setting a tournament record at eighteen-under par. A few weeks later he won the National Collegiate Championship, setting the course record in the process. During his first year in college Tiger earned the Male Freshman of the Year Award at Stanford, and as a sophomore the NCAA named him the College Golfer of the Year.

Tiger is motivated by a long-term goal, which is to become the greatest golfer of all time. His measuring stick is Jack Nicklaus, who is generally recognized as the best golfer to ever set foot on a course. Tiger was not unlike many children who dreamed of becoming the best ever at his or her sport. But Tiger wasn't just dreaming of it, he was planning on it. When Tiger was ten, *Golf Digest* published a list of Nicklaus' achievements, along with his age at the time of each one. That list became a blueprint for Tiger's future in golf.

From the day that Tiger tacked that list onto his bedroom wall, he was on a mission. Even small victories were steps toward his ultimate goal of breaking Nicklaus' records. When their accomplishments are compared by age, Tiger Woods has surpassed all of Nicklaus' records as an amateur and as a young pro. However, what drives Tiger is the number of victories Nicklaus had in major championships. Each year, four majors are played: The Masters, The U.S. Open, The British Open, and the PGA Championship. If a player wins even one major in his lifetime, his career is generally considered a success. Jack Nicklaus won eighteen majors in a professional career that spanned three decades. At the age of thirty-three, Tiger has won fourteen. Many think it's just a matter of time before the inevitable happens, including Nicklaus himself. "He set a goal to break my records," Nicklaus said. "And that's going to stay his goal until he does it. I would be very surprised if he doesn't break my records. Very surprised."

Although it will be quite some time before Tiger Woods conquers all of Jack Nicklaus' records, he has undoubtedly been the most dominant player in the game over the past several years. To make it on the pro tour, a player must either finish as one of the top 125 money winners in the previous year or win a tournament on the PGA tour. This gets tricky—how can a golfer win a PGA tour event if he is not yet a professional? According to the rules, once Tiger initially declared himself a pro, he could receive a maximum of seven special invitations to accomplish one of these feats. Otherwise, he would have to earn his tour card at qualifying school. This is a rare occurrence, and many people doubted this rookie could reach such a lofty goal. Of course, Earl Woods had no doubts. "Giving Tiger seven shots at a tournament, he's going to win one," he said confidently.

In his allotted seven tournaments, Tiger finished in the top ten in five of them and won two, placing him twenty-third on the money list. Not only did he earn the right to play professionally the following year, it was the best stretch of golf played on the PGA tour in the previous fourteen years. He was the first player to finish in the top five in five straight tournaments since 1982. In his professional debut in a major tournament, Tiger won the Masters by twelve strokes. In the process he made history by breaking the all-time tournament record, topping Nicklaus' mark by one stroke. After dismantling his fellow competitors at the Masters, Tiger was not satisfied. When the tournament ended, he watched tapes of himself during the tournament and found multiple flaws in his swing. He called his swing coach, and they spent the next year and a half "fixing" the best swing in the world. People couldn't understand why he was tinkering with perfection, But Tiger Woods was not interested in being the best golfer for 1997. He wanted to be the best golfer of all time. To earn that distinction, he knew he had to always be improving.

To date, Tiger's greatest achievement is that he is the only person to have won four major championships in a row. He did not win them all in the same year, so by definition his wins are not considered a "grand slam." However, his performance was grand enough that people began calling it the "Tiger-slam." Jack Nicklaus called Tiger's four wins "the most amazing feat in the history of golf." Even more remarkable was the manner in which he won those tournaments. Tiger won the U.S. Open by fifteen strokes over the nearest competitor. He broke a record that had stood for 138 years by winning with the biggest margin of victory in a major championship. At the British Open, Tiger won by eight strokes and set a record for lowest score ever in that tournament. In the final major of 2001, Woods shot nineteen under par at the PGA Championship, setting yet another all-time scoring record at that event. In just his fifth year on the tour, Tiger held the record for the lowest total score in all four majors. Ernie Els, the player who often finished second to Woods said, "It seems like we're not playing in the same ballpark right now. When he's on, we don't have much of a chance." Bobby Jones, the man who held many of the amateur records that Tiger broke, simply said, "He plays a game with which I am not familiar."

Tiger's impact on the game of golf is immeasurable. Jake Poe said, "For a game that sometimes people don't consider exciting, he is going to change that. He's going to redefine the game. He already has." It is true—Tiger Woods has made golf cool. Since he entered the PGA tour, ticket sales have skyrocketed, prize money is increasing at a staggering rate, and Tiger has brought a whole new generation of people to the game. When Tiger declares that he will be playing in a certain tournament, tickets sell out almost immediately. The galleries that follow him are enormous, even when he is not in contention.

Many people know that Tiger is currently the highest paid athlete on the planet. His endorsement deals alone are worth hundreds of millions of dollars and he has earned more than $70 million dollars on the PGA tour. What most people don't know is that he has given away every penny that he has ever earned from the PGA. To formally give this money away, Tiger established a charitable foundation in his name. The Tiger Woods Foundation is dedicated to helping kids realize their potential through community programs, grants and responsible parenting. The foundation gives millions of dollars each year to prepare children for success. His father once said proudly, "He's helping kids. He's trying to reverse that 'you're no good' conditioning process that's so prevalent. The ability to dream, and dream big, restores hope." When asked how he wants to be remembered, Tiger says, "Not as a golfer." In other words, he believes that golf is just a vehicle that allows him to make a difference in the lives of others.

With all this success, fame, and money, most people think that Tiger should have no worries. But try to imagine the pressure. Tiger has been the number one golfer in the world for six straight years. He is the only athlete to be named *Sports Illustrated* Sportsman of the Year on two separate occasions. Put another way, if 126 of the world's best golfers enter a tournament, only one can win. Of the 125 who don't win, only Tiger is asked, "What happened? Why didn't you win?" It is the reason he is constantly on the practice range. Tiger once said,

"You have to understand, we [pros] spend our lives on these tees. We're out here four or five hours a day banging balls."

If that isn't enough pressure, also remember that Tiger entered a sport that historically has been considered a white man's game. The Masters Tournament, an event he has won three times, did not even allow blacks to enter until 1975. Not surprisingly, Tiger has had to deal with racism on a number of occasions. After appearing at the Masters Tournament for the first time, he received an anonymous letter that contained the following statement: "Just what we don't need, another nigger in sports." When Tiger was in the midst of winning his first U.S. Amateur title, he was paired against the head coach from the University of Florida. A man from the crowd whispered, "Who do you think these people are rooting for? The nigger or the Gator Coach?" At several tournaments over the years, extra security has been added because of specific threats to Tiger's safety.

The irony is that Tiger's background is a blend of African American, American Indian, Chinese, Thai, Dutch, and Anglo. That is why he refers to himself as the United Nations. Tiger's mother, who was born and raised in Thailand, is understandably upset about the perception that her son is black, "They don't understand," she says. "To say he is one hundred percent black is to deny his heritage...to deny me." Regardless of his diverse heritage, Tiger was branded as the "Great Black Hope" from the time he became a teenager. "It isn't fair," his father said, "but it's realistic and he is cognizant of his role and his image and how he affects others." For some, he is playing for an entire race every time he steps on the course. Even Michael Jordan, the man recognized as the greatest basketball player of all time, understands the significance of a black man playing in a white man's game. "People make comparisons to me," he said, "but Tiger has a lot more weight on his shoulders than I ever had."

So how does Tiger handle this added pressure? He has a clear understanding of history and embraces his heritage. He understands the significance of his efforts, but he also does not let race define him. He does not want to be perceived as a great black golfer or a great Asian golfer; he just wants to be a great golfer. Tiger is guarded when discussing the topic of race and has released only one statement to the media on the subject. In part, he said, "The critical and fundamental point is that ethnic background and/or composition should not make a difference. It does not make a difference to me. The bottom line is that I am an American and proud of it. That is who I am and what I am. Now, with your cooperation, I hope I can just be a golfer and a human being."

Tiger would rather let his actions speak louder than his words on this subject. When he was a nineteen-year-old amateur and had just made the cut at the Masters tournament for the first time, he left the confines of the exclusive Augusta National Golf Club and ventured over the railroad tracks to a not-so-historic, municipal course. He and his father put on a golf clinic there for local black children and held an informal chat with the caddies of Augusta. Tiger wanted to pay his respects to the black men who carried the bags for the club's members. One of the caddies said to him, "It's a great thing for golf, and it's great especially for black youth." Tiger replied, "My dad has always taught me these words: care and share. That's why we put on clinics. The only thing I can do is try to give back."

Perhaps the best testament to Tiger's character was born out of a mistake that he made in 1996. Shortly before he turned pro, Tiger won the U.S. Amateur in a grueling match. Afterward, he was immediately whisked away to the scene of his professional debut. In the meantime, he was negotiating multi-million dollar deals and living off of pure adrenalin. After four weeks on the PGA tour, he decided to withdraw from his fifth tournament, saying that he was mentally exhausted and needed to recharge his batteries. He also decided to skip a dinner that was to be held in his honor as the recipient of the College Golfer of the Year Award. The dinner had been planned for several months and more than 200 people were traveling from all over the country to attend.

Criticism for Tiger's decision to skip the event was intense. Pro golfer Curtis Strange said, "This tournament was one of the seven to help him out at the beginning when he needed help to get his card. How quickly he forgot that." Another well-known player, Peter Jacobson, chimed in. "You can't compare him to Nicklaus and Palmer anymore, because they never did this." Arnold Palmer, one of the best golfers of all time, said, "Tiger should have played. He should have gone to the dinner. The lesson is you don't make commitments you can't fulfill, unless you're on your deathbed.... The important thing is how he handles it from here."

Tiger got the message—loud and clear. He sent a handwritten letter of apology to each and every person who was scheduled to attend the event. He reimbursed the tournament sponsors for the $30,000 they paid to host the dinner, and he politely requested that it be rescheduled for a later date. When he arrived at the rescheduled banquet, he did not dodge the issue. Instead, he took full responsibility for his actions and addressed the audience with these words: "My actions were wrong. I'm sorry for the inconvenience I may have caused. I'll never make that mistake again." And he hasn't. We all need to have enough humility to learn from our mistakes, take full responsibility for our actions, and take steps to right our own wrongs.

Mr. and Mrs. Woods, congratulations! Tiger is indeed an even better person than he is a golfer.

Booker T. Washington

Perseverance

Perseverance—literally a thousand well-known people could have been selected to exemplify this character trait. The ability to overcome obstacles and achieve success is so quintessentially American. The American dream is to take an idea, work hard, and persevere to overcome all obstacles in order to earn a comfortable living. Our system of capitalism embraces this entrepreneurial spirit that says anybody—no matter their gender, race, or religion—can achieve the American dream.

Booker T. Washington was selected to illustrate perseverance because no one else in the history of America overcame more in a given lifetime. He was born a slave, the most degrading condition imaginable. Yet near the end of his life he was an advisor to the President of the United States. His is the real-life story of a slave boy who overcame all odds to become recognized as the most powerful leader of black America from 1895–1915. Washington did more to improve black and white relations in the post-Civil War era than anyone else of that time. How did he accomplish so much when countless others failed? The simple answer is that he set a goal for himself and did not rest until that goal was achieved. Of course, it is more complicated than that, and the story of his life illustrates the hard work, sacrifice, and perseverance he exhibited during his lifetime to achieve his goals.

Booker T. Washington's mother was a cook at a small plantation in Virginia and, like most slaves, worked from sunup to sundown, seven days a week. Washington never met his father and did not even know his name. According to his autobiography, he also did not know the year or month that he was born. At the time little attention was paid to family records of slaves. Nonetheless, Booker was likely born in the spring of 1856. By definition, a black person born before the end of the Civil War was a slave. He was regarded as property, having no legal rights. He was owned in the same manner that a farm animal might be owned today. For the first nine years of his life, Booker lived in a one-room cabin where he slept on the dirt floor with his mother, brother, and sister, using rags as blankets. In our times these living conditions would be considered unthinkable, but they were common among slaves in the rural South.

At that time, it was illegal to educate a black person in the South. The punishment for such an infraction was severe. The only time Booker went to school was to carry the books of the slave master's daughter. He often dreamed of the day that he could learn to read and write. He later wrote, "I had the feeling that to get into a schoolhouse and study in this way would be about the same as getting into paradise." Can you imagine a young child of today having those same thoughts—equating school with paradise?

Booker spent most of his days working. He was not old enough to do hard labor, but his chores included cleaning the yard, carrying water, and fanning the flies away from the slave master's family during mealtime. Booker later recalled, "From the time that I can remember anything, almost every day of my life has been occupied in some kind of labor."

After the Civil War ended in April 1865, the slaves were freed. It's hard to imagine the magnitude the Emancipation Proclamation had for people of color. The thought of freedom brought tears of jubilation and joyous cheers from millions of black people. Of course, many had spent their entire life on plantations and were too old to start a productive life on their own. But this was not the case for Booker. He was only nine years old and had his whole life ahead of him.

However, life was hard in the 1800s for most black people, children included. Booker's family was free, but they were penniless, jobless, and homeless—not a good situation for a mother with three young children. Booker's mother was married to a former slave who lived at another plantation. During slavery they were permitted to see each other only once a year, usually at Christmas. Now that freedom had been declared, Booker's mother could join her husband in West Virginia. The family packed up what little belongings they had and made the 200-mile trek. The automobile had not yet been invented, and the family did not own a horse, so they covered the great distance on foot. To make this trip today by car would take a mere three and a half hours. Yet in 1865, this trip took several weeks. Along the way, the family slept on open ground and cooked what little food they had over log fires.

Upon their arrival, Booker was introduced to his new living quarters. He later wrote, "Our new house was no better than the one we had left on the old plantation in Virginia." Despite Booker's young age, his stepfather had already secured him a job working in the salt mines. He put in ten to twelve hours of physical labor every day in some of the worst working conditions imaginable. Not long after Booker arrived in West Virginia, one of the first schools for black children opened up close to his home. Remembering his vision of "paradise," Booker was eager to learn to read and write. However, his stepfather would not allow him to leave his job and attend school. Booker was determined to not let this decision deter him from his goal. He successfully pleaded with the teacher to give him lessons at night, after he finished his long shift in the mines. After some time under this arrangement, Booker negotiated a deal with his stepfather that would allow him to attend school during the day. Booker was to rise before dawn and work in the mine from 4:00–9:00 a.m. He was then allowed to attend school during the day, only to return to the mines for another two hours in the evening. He was determined to get an education—no matter how hard he had to work or what he had to overcome.

Booker was a quick study and did well in school. He wanted to soak up all the knowledge he could, but it was not long before he knew just as much as the teachers at his local school. He soon heard about a well-respected school for black students in his home state of Virginia. The school was called Hampton Institute, and to Booker, it sounded like heaven. With his natural spirit of determination, he made the decision that he would one day attend Hampton Institute. "I resolved at once to go to that school," he later wrote, "although I had no idea where it was, or how many miles away, or how I was going to reach it... That thought was with me day and night."

At the age of sixteen, Booker set off for Hampton Institute, leaving his family behind. With not much more than the clothes on his back, he began the long journey that stood between him and his future. Even with very little food to eat and no shoes on his feet, he persevered to reach his goal. After many days of travel, Booker reached Hampton with a mere fifty cents in his pocket. He had not bathed in quite some time, his clothes were torn, and he had not eaten anything substantial in days. Still, he did not care. Years later his recollection of the moment he first saw Hampton was as fresh as the day it happened. "The sight of it seemed to give me new life. I felt that a new kind of existence had now begun—that life would now have a new meaning."

The young man's disheveled appearance did not give the sort of impression one wants to make in an interview. The head teacher of the school was not enthusiastic about admitting someone with such an untidy look. She decided to test Booker's resolve and his worth by asking him to clean a room in the school. Booker instinctively knew this was a test and that the outcome of this test would mightily influence his future at Hampton. Needless to say, he cleaned the room as if his life depended on it. He swept the floor three times and dusted the room four times. He moved furniture and removed dust from every nook and cranny in the room. When he was confident that he had done a thorough job, the head teacher began her inspection. She looked everywhere for dirt, but when she was unable to find any, she declared, "I guess you will do to enter this institution."

With no money to pay for his education, Booker took a job as a janitor for the school. To accomplish his job and tend to his studies, he was usually up by 4 a.m. and finished late in the evening with an hour or two of study. His job only paid for part of his tuition, but as he put it, "I was determined from the first to make my work as janitor so valuable that my services would be indispensable." Once again, his hard work and dedication paid off. Despite his inability to cover the cost of his tuition, the school's administrators allowed him to stay for four years to complete his degree.

Even after graduating in 1875, Booker did not consider himself above other people nor did he believe that certain jobs were beneath him. He came away from Hampton Institute with an observation that guided him throughout the rest of his life. "The happiest individuals are those who do the most to make others useful and happy." His life ambition was to help others succeed. He determined that the best way to help others was to become a teacher.

Booker T. Washington took his first teaching position near his former home in West Virginia. He taught during the day, but also opened up a night school for those who had to work during the day. If that weren't enough, Washington taught two Sunday school classes and tutored promising students who had ambitions of attending Hampton Institute. As he had done nearly all his life, he worked 8:00 a.m. to 10:00 p.m. and earned very little pay. However, his good work was recognized. Because his students were so highly prepared once they reached Hampton, Washington was soon asked to return to his alma mater, this time as a teacher. Administrators asked him to start a night school at Hampton. His efforts were met with astonishing success and once again people took notice. In 1881, the president of Hampton Institute, General Samuel Chapman Armstrong, received a letter from a man in Alabama, stating that he wanted to start a college for blacks and was looking for a white person who was qualified to become the first principal of the school, which would be called Tuskegee Institute. General Armstrong, a white man, indicated that he did not know of a white individual with those qualifications, but could recommend Washington to lead this school. Based solely on General Armstrong's recommendation, Washington was hired, sight unseen.

Washington had established a solid reputation by that time. He could be relied upon and was respected by all. Regardless of the size of the task, Washington could be trusted to get the job done. He exercised personal initiative, worked long hours and persevered through many obstacles. At the age of twenty-five, this former slave had become the first black principal of an all-black school in the United States. But Washington was a humble man. His goal was not to become rich or famous, but rather to help people who needed it. He later wrote, "In order to be successful...the main thing is for one to grow to the point where he completely forgets himself; that is, to lose himself in a great cause." For Washington, Tuskegee was that great cause.

Upon arriving at Tuskegee, Washington realized that he had his work cut out for him. He had expected to find a school equipped with books, desks, and other essential teaching materials. He found nothing of the sort. Not only did he not have the necessary tools, he did not have a building in which to teach. During the early days of Tuskegee Institute, Washington taught the first thirty students in an old, run-down church. He had to start with the basics, both in and out of the classroom. As the only instructor, Washington had to teach students how to brush their teeth, wash their clothes, and clean their rooms. He wanted all students to know how to present themselves and make a favorable impression. He also wanted students to learn a trade that would allow them to earn a living once they left Tuskegee. Students learned these trades not by reading about them in books, but by actually doing them. Some students constructed buildings and furniture for the school, while others planted crops and sewed clothing. This physical labor served three purposes. The school desperately needed the resources produced by the students; most of the students needed to trade work for tuition; and students who had learned a trade would add further value to their communities after graduation.

This approach of learning-by-doing continued during Washington's tenure at Tuskegee. All students were required to take part in physical labor, even if they came from well-to-do families. As the school began to expand, Washington hired the best black professionals and educators. Together, the teachers and students designed and completed a variety of projects. Washington led the school by example. He spent portions of his day with an axe in his hands, clearing the property for the next buildings to be built. To raise money for this expansion, everyone participated in fundraising efforts. Teachers and students often sold the goods they produced on campus, but that only generated a small part of the revenue that was necessary for the school's survival. Washington found himself traveling tirelessly around the United States to raise money toward his goal of providing an education to the black students who wanted it. There is no doubt that the driving force behind the success at Tuskegee was Booker T. Washington. He retained his title as principal until he died in 1915.

By the time of Washington's death, Tuskegee had grown enormously. An endowment of $2 million had been established, and over 100 buildings had been built on the campus. The faculty numbered over 200, and they taught forty different majors to the 1,500 students enrolled at Tuskegee. Over the next several years Tuskegee continued to grow in size and reputation. It became even more well known in the 1930s when the U.S. military began training African Americans to become fighter pilots. Tuskegee was selected as the site for this training due to its outstanding aeronautical program. The graduates of this program formed the 332d Fighter Group, thus becoming the first black pilots to fight in combat. During World War II, they fought with distinction. Many of their missions involved escorting U.S. bombers to their designated targets and back. According to war reports, no U.S. bomber was ever lost to enemy fire while being escorted by the Tuskegee Airmen. These pilots were credited with shooting down 251 enemy aircraft during WWII, while losing sixty-six of their own men in combat missions.

Tuskegee Institute has offered much more to the world than well-trained fighter pilots. The Tuskegee VA Hospital opened in 1923, the first hospital operated completely by black professionals. A school of veterinary medicine was also established, and today it produces nearly seventy-five percent of all black veterinarians in the United States. The United Negro College Fund, which has raised over $1 billion in student aid, was also founded at Tuskegee. In 1985, Tuskegee attained university status and now enrolls more than 3,000 students. What an incredible transformation! The school opened in 1881 with one teacher, thirty students, and no buildings. It would be misleading to say that one man is solely responsible for the success of an entire institution, but it is clear that Washington's hard work had an enormous impact on the success of Tuskegee Institute, which in turn has had a positive impact on the lives of millions of Americans.

The irony is that most young people hardly know Washington's name, let alone what he accomplished in his lifetime. While at Tuskegee, Washington was a prominent role model for black Americans. He became an important spokesman for black people and gave speeches that many believe helped to start the healing process between blacks and whites after the Civil War. After making a stirring speech at the Atlanta Exposition in 1895, he was widely referred to as "the most powerful black leader of his time." He became an informal advisor to three U.S. presidents in his lifetime and influenced national policy on race relations. He wrote extensively and authored many books. His most famous is *Up From Slavery*, an autobiography that has been translated into many languages and has sold millions of copies. Like all great leaders, Washington has some critics, but one review of his book from the *Atlantic Monthly* described the book as "A book that...teaches youth to live cleanly, to work honestly, and to love one's neighbor, and to have that long patience which is another name for faith."

Washington was an inspiration and not only to African Americans. He was a shining example of what is possible for all Americans who have initiative, work hard, and persevere through obstacles and setbacks. This is true for students as well as adults—even those students who do not particularly like school and do not see the value of what they are learning in the classroom. However, those who persevere and graduate are usually the ones who get rewarded with better jobs and more money, which allows them to acquire the material items that typically signify success.

It is safe to assume that young Washington did not enjoy getting up at dawn to work in the salt mines or clean classrooms as a janitor. It must have been difficult for him to attend night school after long hours of work. However, like most successful people, he did those things because they were necessary in order to accomplish his goals.

Besides exhibiting perseverance, Washington put forth his best effort in everything he did. As a poor black boy in the South, he did not plan on becoming the principal of Tuskegee Institute or meeting the President of the United States. He merely set out to do the best that he could, every day, without exception. As a boy, he had a dream of becoming educated. While in school, he applied himself and was recognized for his efforts. As a teacher in a small town, he was once again acknowledged for his work, and he was asked to return to Hampton. After establishing a solid reputation at Hampton, he was recommended for the principal's position at Tuskegee Institute. It was only after many years of hard work at Tuskegee that he gained notoriety and accolades from people at the highest levels. The message is clear: If you work hard and do the best you can, you will be rewarded.

The final legacy of Booker T. Washington's life is that it is important to help others who are less fortunate. Almost every facet of Washington's life involved helping others. It's why he became a teacher. It's the reason he accepted the difficult job of starting a school for black students. Washington was compassionate, kind, and his efforts were noble. Just imagine what life would be like if everyone did their part to help their fellow Americans. Washington had every conceivable excuse to become jaded and bitter. As a former slave, he could have easily remained angry at white people for many years. Later in his life, while on a fundraising trip in the Northeast, he was mugged by a white man. He could have held an entire race accountable for this man's actions, but he found the strength to forgive and continued to work to unite blacks and whites throughout his life. Even in his personal life, Washington had a lot to overcome. He was widowed twice, both times after relatively short marriages. He could have turned bitter and lived out the rest of his life alone. Instead, he chose to marry again and loved his third wife until the day he died.

We could all learn a great deal from this man when it comes to perseverance. Washington simply refused to quit. When we meet adversity and things don't go our way, it is often easy to give up or blame others for our failures. That's the easy way out. It might seem tempting, but those who persevere and overcome have much fuller lives. My hope is that you will persevere through the tough and challenging times in your life, only to become a better, stronger person. Perhaps you too will go on to lead a life as full and meaningful as the one led by Booker T. Washington.

Dwight D. Eisenhower

Respect

The date was June 4, 1944. More than one million soldiers from the United States, Great Britain, Canada, and nine other nations were nervously awaiting orders to cross the English Channel and invade Normandy, France. These fighting men had trained many months for this moment. If the allied forces were to defeat Adolph Hitler and his Nazi regime, this invasion, code named Operation Overlord, had to be a success. It was the greatest amphibious assault in the history of warfare. The planning of Operation Overlord took months and involved more than 16,000 soldiers, who pored over every detail of the proposed strategy with painstaking attention. To support the invasion, allied commanders amassed 5,333 ships and 11,000 airplanes.

On the other side of the English Channel, the German military had amassed a wall of defense that Hitler thought was impenetrable—and he had good reason to feel that way. By the end of 1940, the German army had invaded and occupied most of Europe, including France, with little resistance. Germany's main task was to defend the territory it had acquired during the war. From 1940 to 1944, the Germans built the Atlantic Wall. More than 300,000 men were assigned to dig hundreds of miles of trenches, place millions of mines, and put up thousands of miles of barbed wire. Tanks, mortars, and thousands of soldiers armed with every weapon imaginable lined the beaches of Normandy. The Germans were dug into fortified positions composed of concrete and steel. The Germans were ready for a fight, but they did not know when it would come.

The allied commanders, composed primarily of American and British military officers, were to make that decision. The invasion was originally scheduled for June 5. However, on June 3, the day the generals met to execute the order, the weather turned ugly. Stormy conditions were predicted, with strong winds and heavy cloud cover. Such conditions could have been disastrous for the thousands of soldiers storming the beaches of Normandy. The landing craft might be tossed about like toys in a bathtub, killing many of the men before they could even make it to shore. There was also concern about the cover the Air Force and Navy could provide the landing forces, particularly if they could not see their targets clearly. British General Trafford Leigh-Mallory predicted casualties as high as seventy percent for the paratroopers who would be dropped inland on the night preceding the invasion.

The allied commanders, who were some of the most powerful men in the world, debated whether to proceed with Operation Overlord or postpone the invasion. But ultimately the decision was not theirs to make. One man was solely responsible for deciding when to cross the English Channel and invade Normandy. He alone would have to carry the burden if the invasion failed. His name was Dwight David Eisenhower, but everyone knew him as Ike. Just three years earlier, Eisenhower had been a colonel in the U.S. Army, an officer who had never commanded troops nor fought in battle. Yet, in the span of just two short years he rose to the rank of four-star general and was named the Allied Supreme Commander of all European forces—a rise unparalleled in military history. With the fate of the free world at stake, Eisenhower decided to postpone the invasion for twenty-four hours.

The next day, the generals initiated the same debate. The chief meteorologists entered the room of the high command and predicted a thirty-six-hour break in the storm. The debate intensified. Whatever Eisenhower decided, it would be risky, an enormous gamble. Due to the tides on the beachhead, if he postponed the invasion again, the allies would have to wait another two weeks. If another storm hit during that week, the invasion would not be possible until the following year. If Eisenhower went ahead with the invasion and the storm did not break as predicted, the Germans might push the allied forces back into the sea, thereby possibly winning the war. Eisenhower began pacing the room, head down, chin on his chest. He systematically gathered opinions from the other generals. Some were in favor of the invasion. General Walter Smith said, "It's a helluva gamble, but it's the best possible gamble." Bernard Montgomery, the top-ranking British officer, offered more enthusiasm by urging, "I would say—Go!" Others were more skeptical and voiced caution. Air Marshal Arthur Tedder said it was "chancy" and wanted to delay. Admiral Bertram Ramsey was concerned about the Navy's ability to spot its targets with the overcast sky, but he thought the risk was worth taking. Eisenhower calmly weighed the alternatives, and finally said, "I am quite positive the order must be given."

"Okay, let's go." This simple phrase uttered by Eisenhower on June 5, 1944, initiated one of the most successful invasions in the history of warfare. On June 6, 156,000 troops either dropped into Normandy or went ashore on five separate beaches—code named Utah, Omaha, Gold, Juno, and Sword. The fighting that ensued was some of the bloodiest of World War II. Some 2,500 men lost their lives that day, but the beachheads were secured. Hitler's impenetrable Atlantic Wall held up for a mere fourteen hours. More than one million soldiers later entered the war through those very beachheads. Operation Overlord was essentially the beginning of the end of Adolph Hitler and his Nazi regime. In the following year, Eisenhower would oversee the hard-fought victory of the allied forces over Germany, culminating with Hitler's suicide on April 30, 1945.

In years to come, Eisenhower would be appointed president of Columbia University and later named the first Supreme Command of NATO. Others might know him as the thiry-fourth President of the United States who won landslide victories in 1952 and 1956. However, nothing he would later accomplish would compare with the importance of Operation Overlord and the invasion of France. The free world owes General Eisenhower a debt of gratitude for his exemplary leadership during World War II.

The primary question is, how did Eisenhower, a man who was only a colonel in 1941 and had no combat experience, come to be appointed Supreme Allied Commander? The simple answer is "respect"—he gave it and expected it in return. Subordinates and superiors alike had a deep level of respect for the man nicknamed Ike. This did not happen by accident. Eisenhower earned the respect of those around him. In the Army, people often move from post to post and are frequently reassigned to other commanding officers. Eisenhower's philosophy was simple. "My ambition in the Army was to make everybody I worked for regretful when I was ordered to other duty." To accomplish that, he would often work up to eighteen hours a day, seven days a week. He was loyal to his superiors and routinely exceeded their expectations. They knew that Eisenhower was a man who could be trusted. In the 1930s General Douglas MacArthur described Eisenhower as "the best officer in the Army. When the next war comes, he should go right to the top."

When Eisenhower later assumed a top leadership role, he made clear his respect for those he was leading, especially the common foot soldier. In the months preceding D-Day (as that fateful day in Normandy came to be known), Eisenhower spent as much time with the troops as possible. During the spring of 1944 he visited twenty-six divisions, twenty-four airfields, and five war ships. Eisenhower wanted every soldier who would storm the beaches of Normandy to at least get a look at the man who was giving the orders. Even more important, Eisenhower showed a strong interest in the enlisted men as individuals. He would often ask about their hometown, their jobs before the war, and what they planned to do after the war was won. The soldiers admired and respected Eisenhower. Even on the eve of D-Day, Eisenhower paid a visit to 101st Airborne Division. He told a group of enlisted men not to worry about the pending battle. A sergeant from Texas responded, "Hell, we ain't

On June 7, 1944, General Dwight D. Eisenhower visits the secured Normandy beachhead aboard the HMS Apollo. Photo courtesy of the Dwight Eisenhower Presidential Library [65-327-2].

worried, general. It's the Krauts that ought to be worrying now." Eisenhower found a man from Kansas, his own home state, and said, "Go get 'em, Kansas." He asked a young lieutenant from Michigan if he was ready. The lieutenant responded that he had been well trained, well briefed, and was ready to go. A voice shouted from the crowd, "Now quit worrying, general, we'll take care of this thing for you." After many months of careful planning, Eisenhower knew that it was the fighting man who was ultimately responsible for winning the battle.

An important part of Eisenhower's leadership philosophy was this: In victory, spread the wealth; in defeat, accept full responsibility. This philosophy was never more evident than in the moments after Eisenhower made the fateful decision to send the allied troops onto the beaches of Normandy. In a quiet moment, sometime after making the decision yet before the invasion began, he found the time to write the following statement to be used in the event the invasion failed.

Our landings have failed and I have withdrawn the troops. My decision to attack at this time and place was based upon the best information available. The troops, the air and the Navy did all that bravery and devotion to duty could do. If any blame or fault attaches to the attempt it is mine alone.

Eisenhower refused to place the blame on anyone but himself. For this, people respected him.

Other officers respected Eisenhower for his honesty and genuine nature. People were drawn in by his steely blue eyes and welcoming grin. He was modest, deflecting praise and passing it on to his subordinates. Just like a quarterback who throws the winning touchdown pass and later gives all the credit to the receiver with the great hands and the coach who had the brains to call the play, Eisenhower was a very humble man. This trait endeared him to his fellow soldiers and to millions of Americans.

Eisenhower was also respected for his toughness and willingness to make difficult decisions. To win the war, Eisenhower believed a team effort between America and Great Britain was essential. As such, he would not tolerate any fights between soldiers on the same team. On one occasion, an American officer boasted that the Americans would show the British how to fight. Hearing of this incident, Eisenhower summoned the man to his office. The next day the officer was sent back to the States and demoted. Shortly before D-Day, another high-ranking officer with classified information drank too much one evening and began spouting off in a crowded restaurant about the impending invasion. In wartime, this type of behavior was unforgivable. Nazi spies were all over England. If a spy had learned the details of the D-Day invasion in advance, it could have cost many men their lives. Even though the officer was a personal friend, Eisenhower demoted him, relieved him of his command, and sent him home in shame.

Eisenhower was not the type of person to mince words. He was a straight shooter. And while it was not much fun to get a tongue lashing from Eisenhower, everyone knew where they stood with him. People respected him for his straightforward manner. On two occasions Eisenhower even found himself in the awkward position of reprimanding General George Patton, who was a four-star general and Eisenhower's superior for most of his career. Despite the fact that the two men were good friends, Eisenhower felt that duty and obligation outweighed friendship, and he did not allow his personal loyalty to get in the way of making difficult decisions when necessary.

Dwight D. Eisenhower was not the product of wealth and privilege. Born in 1890 in Denison, Texas, he was the third of six boys. His parents had little money. His father worked at a funeral home and his mother was a homemaker. When reflecting on his upbringing, Eisenhower said, "I have found out in later years we were very poor, but the glory of America is that we didn't know it then." Despite having limited means, his parents always encouraged the boys to have high aspirations. "Opportunity is all about you," the boys were told. "Reach out and take it." Eisenhower's family referred to him as Little Ike, while his older brother Edgar was known as Big Ike. Shortly after Little Ike's birth, the family relocated to Abilene, Kansas. School came relatively easy to Little Ike, and he made good grades without a lot of effort. His true passion was sports. He especially loved football and baseball. In reality, he was just an average athlete, but his will to win overcame his lack of talent. Sports were also the venue where his talents as a leader began to emerge. In the early 20th century, there was no such thing as an athletic director at a high school. So Ike took on the responsibility of writing to local schools and scheduling games. He even arranged for the team's transportation by negotiating free rides on freight trains. When he was not in school or playing sports, Ike was working. He did not mind manual labor and was pleased to have a job that provided him with new clothes since it was the only way he could have clothes that weren't hand-me-downs from his older brothers.

As a freshman in high school, while wearing new pants, he fell and scraped his knee. Because he was not bleeding, Ike thought more of the pants than he did of his knee. However, by the next day, infection set in and he began drifting in and out of consciousness. A doctor was called, but Ike's injury did not respond to treatment. The infection began to spread. The doctor recommended that Ike's leg be amputated, saying, "If the poison ever hits his stomach he will die." In response, Ike said, "You are never going to cut that leg off." He made his older brother, David, promise that he would not allow the doctor to take his leg. David made good on that promise by sleeping in the doorway to ensure that the doctor could not get into the room. Ike's stubbornness paid off. Two weeks later, the infection began to clear up, the fever went away, and Ike returned to consciousness. If Ike's leg had been amputated, neither the military academy nor the military would have ever accepted him. That amputation would surely have changed the life of one of the greatest leaders the world has ever known—and maybe the fate of the world itself.

Ike's stubbornness paid off in that situation, but it didn't always help him. He had a bad temper that plagued him during his childhood and adolescence. When Ike was ten, his parents gave his two older brothers permission to go trick-or-treating but refused to allow Ike to go with them, saying he was too young. Ike was consumed with anger. He turned bright red, clenched his fists, and pounded away on the trunk of an apple tree until his fists were bloodied and torn. Ike ran into his room and cried into his pillow for quite some time. Hours later, his mother came into the room to clean up his wounds and provide a little common sense. She told Ike how immature and destructive anger was and how important it was for him to conquer his temper. Years later, Eisenhower wrote, "I have always looked back on that conversation as one of the most valuable moments in my life."

Over time, Ike learned to control his emotions, instead of allowing his emotions to control him. As a general and a president, he prided himself on the ability to stay level-headed in all situations. By doing so, he was able to review all facts relevant to a particular problem, think through possible solutions, and make the most logical decision. It was his ability to remain calm in a crisis that elevated him in rank over other legendary generals. Typically, people do not want a hothead or someone who is a loose cannon as a leader, especially when important decisions need to be made. It was clear that Eisenhower understood this when he wrote, "Anger cannot win, it cannot even think clearly." On another occasion, he said, "I don't get emotionally involved. I can accept a fact for what it is, and I can also accept the fact that when you're hopelessly outgunned and outmanned, you don't go out and pick a fight."

When Eisenhower graduated from high school, he wanted to go to college, but his family had no money to send him. In 1910 there were no student loans, so Eisenhower worked long hours to save enough money for tuition. Much to his surprise, he soon learned that it was possible to get a free education at a U.S. military academy. Eisenhower took the necessary qualifying exam and finished second in the state of Kansas. He was accepted to West Point, where the finest Army officers gained their education. Although Eisenhower hovered around the middle of his class in academics, he ended up in the bottom portion of his class in discipline. At that time, he had a rebellious streak in him that ran a mile wide. Eisenhower said he started smoking cigarettes while at West Point simply because it was forbidden. Being on time or keeping his room clean was never a priority. Because of his behavior, Eisenhower received hundreds of demerits for failing to meet the high standards set for West Point students.

During his sophomore year, Eisenhower became something of a football star. At running back, he led Army to several wins early in the season. The *New York Times* described him as "one of the most promising backs in Eastern football" and the West Point yearbook declared that "Eisenhower could not be stopped" in a victory over Colgate. Unfortunately, in the following game he severely twisted his knee. A later injury resulted in torn cartilage and tendons, thereby ending his athletic career. But, like all people of great character, Eisenhower rebounded. Due to his passion and understanding of the game, the football coach named him coach of the junior varsity team. It was quite an honor for a student to be entrusted with such a position at a major university. In Eisenhower's first leadership role, he performed admirably, foreshadowing the greatness that would come in the future.

Eisenhower's life story would not be complete without mentioning the love, admiration, and respect he had for his wife, Mamie. They met in 1915 on his first assignment as a newly commissioned lieutenant. After five months of dating, he decided that he couldn't live without her. On Valentine's Day 1916, he proposed, and they were married shortly thereafter.

The role of a military wife is a difficult one. In their first thirty-five years of marriage, the Eisenhowers moved thirty-five times. He was often stationed outside of the United States, living in very rugged conditions. Sometimes Mamie would accompany him, but it was not always possible. Even when they were living together, Eisenhower would frequently work fifteen hours a day, even more so during wartime. And the monetary rewards were not great. When they were first married, he earned a paltry $141 per month. Mamie later said she learned to squeeze a dollar so much that she could make the eagle scream—referring to the eagle pictured on the back of a $1 bill.

The Eisenhowers' first child, Doud Dwight, was born the next year and nicknamed "Icky." When he was just three, Icky contracted scarlet fever and died. Years later, Eisenhower wrote, "This was the greatest disappointment and disaster in my life, the one I have never been able to forget completely." The Eisenhowers comforted each other through their grief and later had another son, John Sheldon Doud. Despite financial difficulties, many months spent apart, and the trauma of the death of their son, the Eisenhowers' love endured for more than fifty-two years.

Due to security concerns, telephone calls by soldiers were prohibited during World War II. The only correspondence between Ike and Mamie was in the form of letters—lots of them. Ike wrote Mamie more than three hundred love letters over the course of the war. He would often do so late at night when he missed her most. It provided him with an opportunity to put aside the stress of being supreme commander and just be Ike, her husband. In one letter he wrote, "It's impossible for me to tell you how tremendously I miss you. Your love and our son have been my greatest gifts from life."

Some of the couple's best times were yet to come. Using the campaign slogan, "I like Ike," Eisenhower won lopsided victories to become a successful two-term president. During his tenure in the White House, Eisenhower was widely respected for taking a firm stance against the Communist government in Russia. On the home front, he was also praised for desegregating the U.S. military to ensure that blacks and whites could serve side by side. He ordered troops to oversee the integration of black students into all-white schools in Little Rock, Arkansas. "There must be no second-class citizens in this country," Eisenhower once wrote.

The former general worked hard to achieve world peace during his presidency, saying, "How I wish this cruel business of war could be completed quickly." To that end, he signed a truce that ended the Korean War. He initiated the Atoms for Peace Program and proposed that the United States and Russia exchange aerial photographs of their military establishments as an act of goodwill. In addition to his diplomatic successes abroad, President Eisenhower balanced the U.S. budget and halted inflation. The American people supported these efforts, and Eisenhower became one of only three U.S. presidents whose popularity was greater upon leaving the presidency than it was when he took the office eight years earlier. This is remarkable, considering that he already enjoyed a great deal of public support at the end of World War II, before he entered politics.

After leaving the Oval Office, Eisenhower refused to accept payment for the speeches he gave across the country. He considered it unethical to receive compensation for fame earned as a public servant. Contrast this with today's politicians, who routinely charge thousands of dollars per appearance. Eisenhower preferred to live out his remaining years quietly with Mamie in their retirement home. In the end, he did not see himself as better than any other person in America. He wanted to be buried in the same type of $95 coffin used for common foot soldiers who died in battle.

During his lifetime, Eisenhower served as a role model for all Americans. As a military hero and as President of the United States, he earned the respect of his family, his peers, and millions of people worldwide. He wisely understood that the best way to gain respect was to first give respect to others. He was a humble man who never gloated or sought public recognition. Nonetheless, he was recognized for his achievements at home and abroad. Even today, we can learn a great deal by measuring ourselves against great people of the past such as Dwight D. Eisenhower. He was a person of great character and is deserving of our respect and admiration for his role in American history.

Dwight D. Eisenhower photo at the beginning of this chapter courtesy of the Library of Congress, Prints and Photographs Division [LC-USZ62-117123]

Sherron Watkins

Honesty

Charles Prestwood is a hard-working blue-collar employee who spent thirty-three years of his adult life working in the gas industry. For the last fifteen years of his career, he was a plant operations worker for a company called Enron. He made a decent salary of $65,000 a year and wisely invested a percentage of his income in a retirement account. By the time he retired, he had built a comfortable nest egg of $1.3 million, more than enough to live on for the rest of his life. There was, however, one problem. Nearly all of his investments were tied up in just one company and that was his former employer, Enron.

In late 2001 the news was made public that many top executives at Enron were corrupt and dishonest. Their years of elaborate lies and deception led to one of the largest corporate scandals the world has ever seen. As a result, the company stock fell from a high of $90 a share in December 2000 to less than seventy cents a share just eleven months later. The full impact of this dramatic drop was felt by thousands of Enron employees and retirees, including Charles Prestwood. "I can tell you, without pulling punches, something stinks here," he said during a Congressional hearing called to investigate the Enron debacle. "I lost everything I had." The nest egg he had worked so hard to build was now nearly wiped out.

When Enron filed for the largest bankruptcy in history on December 2, 2001, many Americans suffered enormously. Almost 5,000 employees were fired without warning. To make matters worse, the company promptly cancelled their medical insurance. Without a steady paycheck, many workers could not afford to pay their medical bills. Some cancelled surgeries or could no longer afford to take their prescription drugs. In less than a year, thousands of people lost their income, their health insurance, and their retirement funds. So, what happened? How did such a large and respected company self-destruct so quickly? The simple answer is dishonesty and greed. It took the actions of one courageous employee, Sherron Watkins, to expose this widespread fraud to the rest of the business world.

Initially Kenneth Lay, Enron's chief executive officer, had a superb business plan. He hired the smartest, most energetic people and rewarded them with generous salaries and bonuses. Many people got rich working at Enron, which was named by *Fortune* magazine as one of the "Best 100 Companies to Work for in America." *Fortune* also named Enron America's most innovative company for five consecutive years. In 1996 *Business Week* included Lay in its list of Top 25 Managers of the Year. On paper anyway, Enron was worth billions of dollars, and the company was ranked seventh on the Fortune 500 list.

The corporate culture at Enron, however, was unhealthy. There was immense pressure on employees to close profitable deals at any cost. The motto of one of the executives was "Never say 'no' to a deal." As long as employees produced results, they were not questioned about their methods. CEO Lay even wrote a chapter for a best-selling book in which he emphasized that "rule breakers get to the future first." Enron employees got the message that it was okay to put ethics aside in pursuit of profit. And, sadly, many of them did.

In order to inflate its profits and please industry analysts, Enron began to "cook the books" by using questionable accounting practices. For example, if the company met its projected earnings in a given year, executives would transfer some of the earnings to the next year to cover any unexpected losses. On one occasion, earnings of $70 million disappeared, only to reappear in the next fiscal period. Executives also began inflating the cost of the company's assets. Questionable accounting practices were used routinely but not questioned as long as it was good for business. Enron employees even developed a name for these unethical deals, calling them "Jasons" after the main character in the *Friday the 13th* horror films.

The largest of all of these "Jasons" involved a dummy corporation that was created to buy off some of Enron's debt. In other words, Enron was doing business with itself. Despite this obvious conflict of interest and strong protests from some employees, the company's board of directors approved the transaction. Even worse, the accounting firm charged with overseeing Enron's finances also gave its okay. Why would a reputable accounting firm go along with this unethical proposal? According to records, Enron was paying the firm close to $100 million per year for its services. If the accountants did not go along with this illegal scheme, Enron might fire them. In this case, greed won out over common sense.

For a while, it seemed as if no one at Enron had the courage to protest the widespread corruption at the company. Nobody, that is, except Sherron Watkins. As a vice president at Enron, Watkins was not directly involved in the wrongdoing, but she was able to uncover the truth. Armed with incriminating information, she made a bold decision to expose the illegal activity at Enron. She became a "whistleblower." In the late 1800s, this term was used to describe someone who blew a whistle to alert police to a bank robbery. Watkins did not inform the police of what she uncovered, but she did take her concerns straight to the top. She wrote letters and met personally with Lay, which triggered an investigation into the corruption. Watkins demanded honesty from her employer. For that and for the courage of her convictions, *Time* honored her as Person of the Year for 2002.

Before Sherron Watkins found herself on the cover of *Time*, she was just an average citizen like anyone else. She grew up in the small town of Tomball, Texas. Except for the drilling rigs that drilled for oil within the city limits, Tomball was an unremarkable small town. Sherron's uncle owned the local supermarket, and her cousin managed the funeral home. Her mother, grandmother, and great-grandmother had lived in

Tomball their entire lives. Sherron's parents divorced when she was an adolescent, and she lived with her mother and sister in a modest two-bedroom house. Religion was a large part of Sherron's daily life. She was active in Salem Lutheran Church and attended a Lutheran school before transferring to Tomball High School. She was an excellent student and a member of the National Honor Society. For extra money, she worked as a cashier at her uncle's supermarket.

Sherron wasn't just raised in a small town—she had small town values, too. She understood the value of hard work, was loyal to her family and friends, and understood that it was important to respect authority figures. Above all else, she knew the difference between right and wrong. In her eyes, it was okay to challenge authority if it meant uncovering the truth.

When Sherron was in eighth grade, she had a significant experience that would prepare her for her role at Enron many years later. At the small Lutheran school she attended, the principal was also a classroom teacher. Frequently, he shirked his teaching duties and did not show up to class. Sherron recognized that students were being shortchanged by this situation, and she told her uncles about it. Because they were elders in the Lutheran church, they were in a position to address the situation, and not long after, the teacher left the school. Sherron learned that questioning authority by reporting wrongdoing could result in positive change.

Taking the advice of her mother, Sherron majored in accounting at the University of Texas, where she earned a bachelor's degree in 1981 and a master's degree the next year. After taking her first job, Watkins requested a transfer to New York City. In spite of her small town roots, she wanted to see the world. New York was an exciting place for a young professional. Sherron worked hard, but she played hard too. She had an active social life, traveled extensively, and during the summers she shared a house with a large group of friends in a prestigious area on Long Island called the Hamptons. The fast-paced lifestyle was a lot of fun for a young, single woman, but when she entered her mid-thirties, she decided it was time to return to Texas and settle down. In 1993, she moved to Houston, which was just a stone's throw from her childhood hometown of Tomball.

Watkins soon landed a job at Enron, married a fellow Texan, and gave birth to a daughter, Marion. She was successful at Enron and was promoted to vice president. Everything in her life was going well, until she began to uncover the unethical accounting practices at Enron. She was faced with a number of real-life ethical dilemmas that would prove to have dire consequences for her and thousands of others.

On paper, it is easy to know right from wrong. In the real world, however, things are often more complicated. In Watkins' situation, the crimes she uncovered were being committed by people who wielded a lot of power and could fire her if they chose to. Losing her job would put her family's well being in jeopardy. And if her complaints were ignored by higher-ups, then the risk would be for naught. However, if she did nothing and let the situation continue, she could be considered guilty by association. Watkins knew that her conscience would not let her ignore the situation. In the end, Watkins was not the only person who knew about the fraud at Enron, but she was the only person to come forward and report it.

Watkins worked for several departments during her eight years at Enron. Sometimes her move to another department was due to a reorganization. Other times, Watkins found herself uncomfortable with the business practices in a particular department. When her objections were dismissed, she would look for a different job in another department. It was a solution that allowed her to hold onto her integrity and her job at the same time. At Enron Watkins was known as "Buzzsaw" because of her stubbornness and brutal honesty.

In June 2000, Watkins went to work for Enron Broadband Services. This department was supposed to give Americans a better, faster Internet and was touted as the hottest new initiative at Enron. Broadband Services had just teamed up with Blockbuster to provide movies over the Internet via home computers. The company projected that Broadband would produce revenues of $54 billion in 2000 and $280 billion in

In the wake of the Enron corporate scandal, Sherron Watkins, the infamous whistleblower, testifies before the U.S. Congress. Photo courtesy of Sherron Watkins.

2001. Analysts on Wall Street bought the hype hook, line, and sinker. Enron stock soared as a result—increasing twenty-five percent in one day. By the end of 2000 the stock was worth over $90 per share, an increase of forty-eight percent in a matter of a few short months.

There were, however, a few problems with this success story. The company was spending millions and millions of dollars, but Broadband was generating very little revenue in return. In fact, by the end of 2000, Broadband had 900 employees, yet only 300 customers had signed up for the service. With those numbers, for the company to make money customers would have to pay $700 per movie—not exactly a smart business plan. Furthermore, almost all of the 900 employees had spent their careers in the energy sector and did not have the necessary qualifications to be working for an Internet provider. Soon it became apparent that virtually no one knew what they were doing. As a seasoned professional, Watkins realized she had made a big mistake by joining the department.

Even though Broadband's losses began to mount, Enron's annual report did not reflect these losses. Watkins wondered how that could be. After doing some investigating on her own,

Watkins discovered that Enron was part of "the worst accounting fraud I've ever seen." Numbers were being manipulated, losses were being disguised, and people were covering it up. Watkins also discovered the "Jason" deals that kept hundreds of million of dollars off the books. Instead of reporting these staggering losses, Enron reported $425 million in earnings for the first three months of 2001. Watkins knew something was wrong. Senior executives were selling their own stock in the company as fast as they could. One executive personally made over $33 million from selling stock in a span of just eight months. A Wall Street analyst later said that Enron was flunking the smell test— the numbers just did not add up.

Because Watkins had a master's degree in accounting, she was able to figure out who was behind the corrupt practices at Enron and who was covering them up. She decided to blow the whistle on those involved. She initially wrote a letter to CEO Ken Lay. She believed that if he knew what she had uncovered, he would remedy the situation and save the company. She was sure that he would do the right thing. In her letter, she laid out the evidence and warned him, "I am incredibly nervous that we will implode in a wave of accounting scandals." She wanted assurances that he would investigate her findings and make appropriate changes. Lay responded by asking a few top executives to look into the allegations, and in return, they told him there was nothing to worry about.

Watkins became more determined than ever to stop the fraud at Enron. She set up a meeting with Lay. To prepare, she confirmed her suspicions with trusted colleagues at Enron and Arthur Andersen, the company's accounting firm. She did her homework to ensure her facts were accurate. In the process, she also exposed herself as a whistleblower. Being a whistleblower is a lot like being a tattle-tale—and no one likes a tattle-tale. Texas law provided no protection for whistleblowers, meaning that Watkins could be fired very easily. Still, she wanted to come forward because she was convinced that it was the right thing to do. According to her mother, "[Sherron] knew she had to say something. But all along, she never imagined that she was going to be the only one." Jessica Uhl, a coworker, praised Watkins' courage, saying, "She had the sense of conviction to do what she did, and the ability to articulate what needed to be said."

Watkins met with Lay, presenting the facts as best she could. She wrote a second, longer letter that chronicled all the irregularities occurring at Enron. She even proposed specific steps for Enron to follow if the company hoped to get out of this mess. She advised the company executives to come clean about Enron's corrupt accounting practices and make assurances that this type of unethical behavior would never occur again. She noted in her letter that these steps would have severe consequences for the company, but complete honesty was the only plausible way to save the business. When the meeting ended, Watkins felt relieved and proud at the same time. She said, "There was a feeling that I had done the hardest thing in my life, but I had carried the torch and dropped it off."

Lay immediately confronted the key person Watkins implicated in the scandal. After hearing the allegations, the man demanded that Watkins be fired immediately. However, Lay would not allow it. In fact, Lay was so astonished by this reaction that he launched a full-blown investigation. Watkins was sure that Lay would take positive steps to help Enron regain the trust of the American people. To her surprise, he continued to hide the truth. In a speech in September 2001, Lay said, "Our third quarter is looking great. We are continuing to have strong growth in our businesses." He even tried to recruit new investors, saying, "My personal belief is that Enron stock is an incredible bargain at current prices." He made this statement about the same stock that he was selling as fast as he could—and making millions of dollars in the process.

Nobody knows whether Enron would have been able to survive if the company had followed Watkins' recommendation to tell the truth. The top executives continued to lie, and once their lies were exposed, no one trusted them. Without trust, Enron had zero credibility. Business partners, investors, and banks refused to do business with the company. Enron executives were charged with hundreds of counts of fraud. As a result, Enron declared bankruptcy, thousands of people lost their jobs, and employee retirement accounts were decimated.

When the government launched an investigation of Enron to figure out what went wrong, only one person received praise from members of the U.S. Congress. Representative Cliff Stearns had this to say to Sherron Watkins: "I believe that employees such as yourself, in no small measure, contribute to the integrity of our commercial system by insisting that all participants play by the rules. And I think all Americans thank you for what you did." Representative Bart Stupak recognized her courage by saying, "Many of my colleagues and I truly appreciate your brave actions..." Representative Richard Burr commented on Watkins' integrity. "I'd add one more uniqueness about Ms. Watkins that was lacking in all the other individuals who have chosen to come before this committee to stop the bleeding at Enron—a moral compass," he said. "You're doing this committee and your fellow Enron employees a great service." Finally, Representative Billy Tauzin referred to Watkins as a role model for the next generation of businessmen and women. "I hope that sons and daughters of American citizens follow your example, frankly, and adopt your concept of corporate loyalty as a mantra."

When Watkins' fellow employees learned of her efforts to confront the management at Enron, many demonstrated their support. Laid-off employees even created a T-shirt that read, "Sherron Watkins, Our Hero." She received hundreds of e-mails, voice mail messages, cards, and letters expressing gratitude for her actions. Some of these messages came from former employees, some came from famous people, and some came from complete strangers all across the country.

Watkins also received national awards for her honesty and courage. She was given the Scales of Justice Award by Court TV and the Women Mean Business Award from Business and Professional Women/USA. Watkins shared her *Time* Person of the Year award with two other honest citizens—Coleen Rowley of the FBI and Cynthia Cooper of WorldCom. The cover of the magazine read simply, "The Whistleblowers." The article described the honesty, courage, and character exhibited by these three women. "They took huge professional and personal risks to blow the whistle on what went wrong at WorldCom, Enron and the FBI—and in so doing helped remind us what American courage and American values are all about."

Together, these women demonstrate the importance of confronting wrongdoing and standing up for the truth. Congress has now recognized the need for whistleblowers in the workplace and has passed legislation to protect those who come forward to expose unethical practices. This protection will help to encourage the next generation of Americans to have the courage to hold themselves and others accountable to a higher standard.

Watkins says she has some regrets. If she had to do it all over again, for example, she says she would have taken her concerns outside the company. She was naïve to believe that the top executives would do the right thing.

To help other companies avoid Enron's mistakes, Watkins has started her own consulting firm to advise businesses on ethics in the workplace. She believes that her story can serve to help others and hopes that she can be a role model for those in the business world. Because of her honesty and the courageous role she played at Enron, she is in high demand as a speaker and consultant. Her popularity proves that "honesty is still the best policy."

Jesse Ventura

Integrity

We all know that integrity is a positive character trait, but what does it really mean to be a person with integrity? Integrity comes from an internal value system that is based upon honesty, fairness, and ethical principles. An individual with integrity uses those core values as a constant guide in making decisions. Unwilling to compromise those values, a person of integrity is less susceptible to corruption and temptation. He or she is motivated to do the right thing, despite easier options. Time after time, a person with integrity chooses to do what is right over what is popular. In other words, people with integrity live out their belief systems in their everyday behavior. When someone says, "You are a person with integrity," he or she is saying a lot about your character.

In some ways, Jesse Ventura is a controversial choice for a book about character. He grew up in the 1960s, as part of the most rebellious generation of the 20th century, and he embraced being a rebel. As part of his counter-culture ways, he experimented with sex, drugs, and rock 'n' roll as a teenager. He ran around with a group of friends he affectionately calls The South Siders. They were a rowdy group that sometimes sneaked out at night, played practical jokes on each other, and had an uncanny knack for finding trouble. Ventura explains, "We weren't juvenile delinquents; I wouldn't put it that way. We just had a streak of mischief in us." But most people would agree that Ventura still is somewhat of a hellion. He is independent by nature and not afraid to speak his mind. He is well known for his controversial statements, and he has been criticized for being too outspoken. Ventura says, "I found out the hard way that whenever you take a stand on an issue, no matter how insignificant, people will line up around the block to kick your ass over it. By having an opinion, you make yourself a target." Standing up for one's beliefs requires courage and integrity, particularly in the face of strong criticism.

Ventura first came into public view as a professional wrestler during the 1970s and early 1980s. Because he worked out regularly and was so muscular, he was dubbed Jesse "The Body" Ventura. Pro wrestling has always been more about entertainment than sport, and Ventura was all about entertainment. He embraced wrestling's "bad boy" persona, dressing in a trademark feather boa, wraparound shades, and tights. With his long bleached-blond hair and in-your-face attitude, he did not project the typical image of a future governor. As one of the villains in professional wrestling, he was expected to work the audience at each match into a frenzy by screaming and yelling at them and at his opponents. In the world of pro wrestling, the more arrogant and obnoxious a wrestler can be, the more successful he can become. Jesse Ventura was one of the best at this shtick, and pro wrestling fans loved to hate him.

When Ventura retired from wrestling, he took his outrageous personality into the announcer's booth and became a wrestling commentator, earning the nickname Jesse "The Mouth" Ventura. He frequently sided with the villains of the sport, and he became even more popular for his on-air personality than he had been for his persona in the ring. Not long after hosting Wrestlemania, he became the color commentator for the Minnesota Vikings and the Tampa Bay Buccaneers. He eventually took his talents to the airwaves, hosting his own "shock" talk radio show. He also had a relatively successful acting career, appearing in films such as *Predator, Running Man, Demolition Man* and *Major League 2,* and on television in *The X-Files* and *Hunter.* Ventura even had a brief stint as the lead singer in a rock 'n' roll band called Soldiers of Fortune.

During Ventura's rise in popularity, many people failed to understand that his outrageous persona was really just a fabrication—a role he played on stage, albeit convincingly. Professional wrestling is not like most sports where the best athlete or best team usually claims victory. In pro wrestling, the people behind the scenes dictate the winner of a wrestling match long before the wrestlers ever hit the mat. If a wrestler wants to continue "winning," he must be entertaining enough to persuade fans to buy tickets. Ventura successfully developed a persona as "The Body," and for that reason, many people pigeonholed him as a half-crazed jock, refusing to believe that he was capable of anything more.

However, Ventura has a multi-faceted personality and continually proves that he is capable of achieving anything he sets his mind to. The foundation for his strong character was established when he was a boy growing up in Minnesota. Jesse Ventura was born in 1951 into a loving and supportive family. He credits his father for his independent streak and says he inherited his ability to stand on his own two feet from his mother. While in high school, he was an all-state swimmer and took advanced classes to prepare for college. However, shortly after graduating, he decided to follow in his brother's footsteps and enlist in the U.S. Navy.

While in boot camp, Ventura was intrigued by a presentation he heard from the Navy SEAL Special Forces. Members of the Special Forces explained that soldiers who joined them could expect to be physically and mentally tested beyond belief. Ventura liked a challenge and had an unusual rationale for wanting to join the Special Forces. "I had a dreadful fear of heights that I wanted to conquer," he explained. Ventura found the courage to face his fears and volunteered for the elite unit. Typically only one out of three Navy SEAL recruits makes it through the intense training, which culminates in "hell week," a seven-day training exercise held without sleep. Ventura was one of thirty-eight young soldiers who made it through the training. As a member of the Navy SEALs, he served two tours of duty in the Vietnam War. Despite his typically outspoken nature, even today he refuses to talk about his experience in Vietnam. He says that he was given a direct order by a commanding officer not to discuss what he did or saw during the war, and he continues to honor that order. Ventura should be admired for his patriotism to this great country and for his service in the armed forces.

Ventura was honorably discharged from the military in 1973 and began to prepare for a career in professional wrestling. Not many people know that Ventura's real name is James Janos. Like many entertainers, he changed his name when his wrestling career took off. Did you actually think that Hulk Hogan and Roddy Piper were real names?

Ventura has an uncanny knack for achieving success in so many different arenas. Because of hard work, an entrepreneurial spirit, and a strong sense of determination, Ventura has always landed on his own two feet. The word "can't" is not in his vocabulary. When he started talking about entering politics, however, he encountered much skepticism and doubt. He says that he never planned on entering politics, but instead politics sort of landed in his lap.

In 1990, when he was thirty-nine, Ventura was living in Brooklyn Park, Minnesota, with his wife and two children. There were a handful of undeveloped lots in the Venturas' neighborhood, and developers proposed building on the property and adding curbs, gutters, and storm sewers. Local residents thought these so-called improvements were unnecessary, especially since they would be paid for with taxpayer dollars. Brooklyn Park citizens gathered 450 signatures for a petition that was presented to the city council. Despite strenuous objections from most of the residents, the council voted unanimously to approve the developers' request. It seemed as if the elected officials did not care about the opinions of their constituents.

After doing some research, Ventura discovered that most of the council's previous votes were also unanimous, but seemed to go unanimously against the will of the people. These same elected officials were spending taxpayer money on golf courses and posh clubhouses. It appeared that council members, while claiming to represent the city's residents, most often made decisions to directly benefit themselves. Their hypocrisy infuriated Ventura. "I wasn't going to take that," he said. "I started attending more and more meetings and getting angrier and angrier." When a council seat opened up, Ventura and others from the neighborhood decided to change things by electing someone who represented the voice of the people. Brooklyn Park resident Joe Enge was elected to the council, but the council's votes still came down 6-1 on most issues. While attending a city council meeting one evening, Ventura gave an impromptu speech about the mismanagement of the city. He looked at six blank faces and said, "You're going to make me run, aren't you?" The council members laughed and said those fateful words they would live to regret: "You could never win."

To defeat the incumbent mayor of twenty-one years, Ventura knew he had to work hard. He launched a grassroots effort to inform the public about the vast corruption in their city government, and he laid out a plan to correct the problem. His straightforward, no-nonsense approach struck a chord with voters. Typically fewer than ten percent of the population turned out for a local election, but Ventura had a way of inspiring the people to get out and vote. In the previous election, 2,500 citizens had voted. In this election, 25,000 people voted, most of them for Ventura. Brooklyn Park is the sixth-largest city in Minnesota and Ventura won in all twenty-four of the city's precincts. The people had spoken. Jesse Ventura was mayor of Brooklyn Park.

Even after his election, however, the council votes usually came down 5-2 against the citizens' interests. Ventura wanted Brooklyn Park residents to see how the "good old boys" operated firsthand, so he began televising the council meetings. It worked. When the council began debating a hot topic, people descended on city hall to voice their opinions. That is the way democracy is supposed to work, Ventura believed. He said, "The only way the system will ever change is if enough well-meaning private-sector people get involved in their local government for the right reasons." He also learned another important lesson in his four-year battle with the entrenched council members "When you have the courage to stand up and tell it like it is," he said, "good people will come out of the woodwork to get behind you."

People began to regard Ventura as a natural leader and a man of integrity. He came to be known as someone who was willing to stand up to the establishment and fight for his convictions. The "establishment," or career politicians, usually are candidates from the Democratic and the Republican parties. Typically, to be elected to state or national office, politicians have to align themselves with one party or the other. They often make promises to big business, unions, or other special interest groups in order to gain their support. These groups then make financial contributions to fund campaigns and influence people to vote for their chosen candidate. In return, once elected, politicians vote in ways that benefit these special interest groups. By doing so, they increase their chances of getting re-elected.

Another consequence of the two-party system is that Republicans align themselves with other Republicans, and Democrats align themselves with other Democrats. In other words, they make deals, such as "If you vote for my bill, I'll vote for yours." Politicians generally vote along party lines because they are indebted to their fellow party members. This trend in politics often leaves a bad taste in the mouths of many Americans, which might explain why people often do not have a lot of faith in the political system. It is also one of the reasons that nearly half of American adults do not vote.

Many well-intentioned people enter politics for the right reasons, but the pressure to conform to certain views is overwhelming. It takes a person of exceptional integrity to refuse to compromise his or her beliefs just to win votes or to please party members. Ventura is that type of person. "No one owns me. I come with no strings attached," Ventura proudly proclaimed.

For that reason, he was asked by the newly emerging Reform Party to run for governor of Minnesota. He initially declined, but then changed his mind due to the state budget situation in Minnesota. Every state has a budget to run the government. Tax dollars are used to educate children, fight crime, pay state employees, and provide other important services to the public. In 1997, the state of Minnesota collected $4 billion in excess tax revenue. In other words, the government overcharged the people. Instead of returning that money to taxpayers, the state's leaders spent it on new programs and high-profile projects that would help them get re-elected.

Angered at this turn of events, in January 1998 Ventura announced that he would run for governor. Many people thought it was just a publicity stunt to rejuvenate his career. Few took him seriously. A common joke was, "What's he going to do, body-slam legislators when they get out of line?" But Ventura was serious and he knew how to win. He touted himself as a working man with common sense ideals. To enhance his image, he adopted a new nickname: Jesse "The Mind" Ventura. He did not pay attention to the latest polls to tell him what to think about certain issues, nor did he conform to party lines. He spoke openly and honestly about what he believed. Throughout the campaign, Ventura never used a single note card in his public appearances. When he was faced with a question he could not answer, he would say, "I don't know, but if it's important, I'm a quick learner—I'll find out."

The rebellious nature that frequently got Ventura into trouble as an adolescent served him well as the anti-establishment candidate for governor. His campaign slogan was "Retaliate in '98." While his opponents appeared boring and pre-packaged, Ventura was a breath of fresh air. Instead of wearing the usual suit and tie, he wore jeans and a Minnesota Timberwolves jacket.

First and foremost, Ventura was committed to remaining true to himself. He refused to be somebody he wasn't. His opponents spent more than $13 million dollars collectively on their own campaigns, most of it coming from big business and special interest groups. Ventura's campaign spent only $600,000, half of which came from a public subsidy and the other half in the form of small checks from ordinary citizens. The turning point in the campaign came during the debates. The other two candidates attacked each other in the usual partisan ways, sounding like any other Democrat and Republican from around the country. Ventura stayed above the fray and spoke directly to the people of Minnesota. He talked about his views and what he intended to do about important issues. People responded to him because he was genuine and forthright. He exhibited integrity, and as a result, he earned their trust.

On Election Day, the media were calling the race a statistical dead heat. As results began to come in early in the day, Ventura was initially behind. As the day wore on, however, he took a slight lead. At five minutes to midnight, Ventura had thirty-seven percent of the vote, compared to thirty-four percent and twenty-eight percent, respectively, for his challengers. Excitement began to mount and people congregated outside of Ventura's campaign headquarters. They soon formed a mosh pit—passing bodies over their heads as if it were a rock concert. As Ventura would say later, "I'm the only candidate in the world who's had three or four mosh pits going on at their election party." Minutes later the three major news affiliates declared Jesse Ventura the next governor of Minnesota. Congratulatory phone calls from the other two candidates soon followed, and after they conceded the race, Ventura's victory was official.

When the news hit the other forty-nine states, most people were stunned. Very few people outside of Minnesota had followed the campaign and most were not familiar with Jesse "The Mind" Ventura. What they knew was an outrageous ex-wrestler, the arrogant ex-commentator, and the brazen former actor. Members of the media were scratching their heads, wondering how the people of Minnesota could have possibly elected such a character. But the people of Minnesota had not been fooled or bamboozled. They were informed voters who had become familiar with Ventura's values, his views, and his character. When Ventura was asked how he won the election, he said, "If I had to pick one reason Minnesotans voted for me, I would have to say that it is because I tell the truth. I stand tall and speak freely, even when it isn't politically expedient to do so." More than that, he made politics seem cool and inspired the average citizen to vote. Approximately sixty-one percent of the state's citizens voted in the election, which was the highest turnout ever for an off-year election. Ventura was able to find a niche with the young, disenfranchised voter. He became the first member of the Reform Party to win a statewide election.

Once elected, Governor Ventura did a number of things that are uncommon for politicians. First, he kept his campaign promises, which included giving back the tax rebate that he felt was duly owed to the citizens of Minnesota. On average, each citizen received a check for $600, the largest rebate the nation had ever seen. Second, he made it clear that he did not intend to be a career politician. Instead, he said he wanted to serve as governor and then return to the private sector, which is what he did in 2002 after his term ended. He encouraged other well-intentioned citizens to follow in his footsteps as well.

Third, he tried to keep the citizens of Minnesota informed in a variety of ways. During his first year as governor, he wrote a book that outlined his personal and political views, which allowed the public to learn where he stood on various issues. He began holding town hall meetings on the Internet and hosted a radio show called *Lunch with the Governor*. His goal was to make state government more accessible to the people. Fourth, the governor set clear boundaries between the job and his family. He declared that he was not going to take calls on Sundays, and he made it clear that he would not allow the job to interfere with his family life. As Ventura put it, "I don't want to come home in four years to a house full of strangers." Finally, he tried to bring a sense of humor to politics, something he thought was sorely missing.

Ventura enjoyed the highest job-approval rating of any governor in the history of Minnesota. As a result, he was courted by the Reform Party to run for president of the United States. In response he said, "I won't say absolutely not, but I wouldn't put any money on there ever being a Jesse 'The Prez' Ventura." He has made it clear that he would not enjoy the personal restrictions that would come with the job. As governor, Ventura had security personnel with him twenty-four hours a day. However, when he retired, the security guards moved on to the next governor. As president, he would have security guards for life, even after leaving office. He has said that is too big a price to pay for himself and for his family.

When people ask why Jesse Ventura should be considered a role model, the answer is always the same. Ventura has integrity and is a man of his convictions. When the rulings of the local politicians in Brooklyn Park, Minnesota, were inconsistent with the will of the people, he did not just complain about it, nor did he bury his head in the sand and ignore the situation. He got involved in the political process and fought against the corruption that he saw in city government. During neither of his political campaigns did he sell himself out to win votes. He ran campaigns that were honest and genuine. Once in office, he continued to communicate with his constituents, and he kept his campaign promises. He voted the issues up or down based on their own merit, not by listening to the polls. He used his own values to guide him to do the right thing on behalf of the people he represented.

Ventura is one of the few individuals who fought the system and won. He showed America that honesty wins over propaganda and having integrity is more important than taking the popular, predictable road. Many politicians, for example, lie about or downplay their youthful indiscretions to fit a certain image. Ventura refused to misrepresent himself just to get elected. He told the truth regardless of what others might think of him.

The story of Jesse Ventura should be an inspiration to all adolescents who have doubts about their ability to be successful in life. At the end of his autobiography, *I Ain't Got Time to Bleed*, Ventura delivers a powerful message about responsibility, personal initiative, and perseverance to the youth of America. He writes, "That's what I want to tell this new generation: take responsibility for your actions. If you make a bad choice, by God pull up your bootstraps and live with it. When you go through life accepting responsibility and working through the tough times, you develop a solid, reliable core inside yourself that's called character."

Finally, he leaves us with these words: "The American dream is still there. You can still work hard for your dream and achieve it.... I'm living proof that dreams can come true. I'm no more special than anyone else. And if I can become governor, so can you!"

Amelia Earhart

Courage

In an era when driving a car was thought to be unladylike, Amelia Earhart was doing barrel rolls in her own two-seater airplane. While most women were tending to the laundry and the dishes at home, she was setting high-altitude and long-distance records in the sky. At a time when women wore only skirts or dresses, she preferred wearing her faded leather coat, khaki pants, and goggles. In fact, when she purchased her first leather coat, she slept in it for weeks to give it a worn look. Earhart never really cared about the traditional role of a woman. She wanted to live life to the fullest and be able to look back and say, "I have no regrets." If she saw a challenge, she wrapped both arms around it and didn't let go until she conquered it.

The challenge that Earhart embraced most enthusiastically was flying. For those of you who are picturing a comfortable Boeing 747, just remember that the "friendly skies" were still decades into the future. At the time Earhart learned to fly, aviation was less than twenty years old. It was in 1903 that Wilbur and Orville Wright recorded the first flight in history at Kitty Hawk, North Carolina. The flight lasted all of twelve seconds and covered 120 feet. The field of aviation progressed in many ways before Earhart took up flying in 1920; however, flying was still considered extremely hazardous. Pilots were routinely killed in accidents, and the thought of a large group of passengers traveling in a plane from one place to another was considered suicidal. Flying was only for the courageous—and certainly no place for a woman, many thought. However, Earhart challenged every notion of what a woman should be. In so doing, she blazed a trail for all women to follow. If Amelia Earhart could be a pilot, which was unthinkable for a female, then other women could be doctors, engineers, or lawyers. She always believed that women were equal to men, and as her life progressed, she proved it. Her story was then, and is now, an inspiration to women who have been told "it's a man's world."

Earhart's progressive beliefs began at home in Atchison, Kansas, where she was born in 1897. Her sister, Murial, arrived two years later. The Earhart girls were raised to believe that they were capable of doing anything that boys could do. This belief was expressed in subtle, yet important ways. Amelia and Muriel were encouraged to go fishing, play baseball, climb trees, and hunt wild game. Getting dirty was considered an essential part of growing up. Unlike other neighbor girls, the Earharts were not limited to wearing dresses or playing with dolls.

Amelia developed into a self-confident, independent, and courageous young woman. She was admired for these traits later in life, but during her childhood, she was often ridiculed for being different. Her home life added to her difficulties. Due to a drinking problem, Amelia's father frequently lost his job and had to move the family to a different town to find employment. After leaving Kansas, the family lived in Iowa, Minnesota, and Missouri. Amelia finally graduated from high school in Illinois. Despite the frequent moves, she was an excellent student with high grades. She attributed part of her success to a practice she began as a young child. She kept and treasured a scrapbook of women who achieved greatness in fields traditionally dominated by men. These women became her role models, inspiring her to become a better person. Socially, Amelia was somewhat of a loner in high school. The caption in her yearbook described her as "The girl in brown who walks alone."

Amelia loved to read and even occasionally wrote poetry, but college was not a good fit for her. It could have been because the preparatory school she attended did not allow her to explore the areas in which she was interested. She wanted to study politics and women's rights, but in 1917 neither of these were part of the curriculum for girls. Amelia was like a square peg that was not about to be forced into a round hole.

When World War I broke out, she took a break from college and became a nurse's aide. While caring for wounded soldiers, she was inspired by their heroic tales. Some of these men were pilots who fought the enemy in the sky. At that time, pilots actually fired at enemy pilots with hand-held machine guns and used hand grenades for bombs.

When the war ended, Earhart wanted to continue helping people. She decided to become a doctor and enrolled in a pre-med program at Columbia University. "But," as she would later write in one of her books, "after a year of study I convinced myself that some of my abilities did not measure up to the requirements which I felt a physician should have." Earhart would have to find another way to make her mark on the world. She went on to hold several different jobs. She worked at a telephone company, developed film for a photographer, and taught English to foreign college students before becoming a social worker at the Denison House, a home for immigrants struggling to adjust to life in the U.S. Earhart found fulfillment as a social worker and even moved into the Denison House to dedicate herself more fully to this profession. However, social work could never compete with the thrill of flying a plane, and she decided that aviation was her true purpose in life.

On December 28, 1920, Amelia Earhart was formally introduced to flying. She was twenty-three when her father took her to a stunt-flying exhibition in Los Angeles, California. After being bitten by the flying bug while listening to the stories of World War I pilots, she was now ready to see these planes in action. As the stunt planes flew overhead, a curious thing happened. A single plane broke formation and made a beeline toward the crowd. Earhart had a strange reaction. Instead of running like most of the people, she courageously stood her ground. At the last second, the pilot turned away, missing Earhart by the narrowest of margins. Instead of being afraid, Earhart was mesmerized by the beauty and the speed of flying.

She later said, "I did not understand it at the time, but I believe that little red airplane said something to me as it swished by."

Later that day, Earhart confided in her father, "Dad, you know, I think I'd like to fly." Mr. Earhart obliged his daughter's fancy and scheduled a flying session for her. The pilot agreed to take her up in his plane under one condition—another pilot had to sit beside her. She understood the meaning of this restriction and later wrote, "I was a girl—a 'nervous lady'. I might jump out. There had to be somebody on hand to grab my ankle as I went over." The pilot's attitude was typical of society's view of women at the time, but Earhart refused to be intimidated by such comments. She was not about to let a little thing like fear stand in the way of her dream of flying. The short flight only confirmed what was already in her heart. "By the time I had got two or three hundred feet off the ground," she exclaimed, "I knew I had to fly." When she returned to the ground, Earhart knew exactly what she was going to do with the rest of her life. The challenge would be making it happen.

As fate would have it, Neta Snook, one of a handful of female pilots in the country, owned a flying school in Los Angeles. Earhart immediately signed up for flying lessons and had her heart set on becoming a licensed pilot. To pay for the expensive lessons, she took on two jobs. Because she understood the inherent danger, she took her flying lessons very seriously. Earhart was not interested in the stunt flying that was so popular at the time, but she insisted on learning a few acrobatic maneuvers. She would not fly solo until she felt confident that she could handle any situation that might arise during flight. In 1921 she became a licensed pilot. Only a few months later, she went up for a leisurely flight and broke a world record by flying higher than any woman ever had—14,000 feet. She would later increase this mark by soaring to 15,000 feet and again later to 18,415 feet.

Earhart loved flying so much that she bought herself a plane for her twenty-fifth birthday. It was a two-seater biplane with an open-air cockpit that allowed her to feel the wind in her face and the bugs in her teeth. The plane was painted bright yellow—her favorite color—and she named it *The Canary*. Like all pilots of her day, Earhart had her fair share of accidents in *The Canary*. The most common type of crash in those days occurred when the nose of the plane flipped over. This would happen when the plane stopped suddenly, usually after landing. This "nosing over" created quite a jolt for the pilot and usually caused minor damage to the plane. Earhart described one of these experiences: "On one occasion I landed in a mattress of dried weeds five or six feet high, which stopped me so suddenly that the plane went over on its back with enough force to break my safety belt and throw me out." She went on to nonchalantly refer to these minor crashes as "the flat tires of flying" and "incidental."

The more serious injuries usually happened during flight. On one such flight, Earhart struggled to get her plane over some trees that stood between her and the runway. She pulled back hard on the stick, which unfortunately caused the engine to stall. The plane crashed hard into a field below, seriously damaging the propeller and landing gear. She referred to the crash as an "interesting experience." Nothing seemed to rattle Earhart. No matter how casual she might have been about the dangers of flying, these crashes were real and potentially deadly.

Unfortunately for Earhart, finances became tight and she reluctantly decided to sell *The Canary* to a former World War I pilot. After buying the plane, the new owner invited a friend to join him for a leisurely flight. Once up in the air, he began to show off for those on the ground. "Suddenly, on one vertical bank the plane slipped," recounted Earhart. "That was the end of it. Both men were killed. It was a sickening sort of thing because it was so unnecessary."

Despite the hundreds of people who died during the infancy of aviation, several significant advances did occur. The most notable took place in 1927 when Charles Lindbergh became the first person to fly solo across the Atlantic Ocean in his plane, the *Spirit of St. Louis*. Earhart marveled at this accomplishment and hoped to one day accomplish such a glorious feat. Four women had previously attempted to cross the Atlantic—all of them perished in their attempts. In total, seventeen pilots had attempted the crossing and failed. Now it was Earhart's turn to try. She knew the risks involved, but just the chance of succeeding was worth it. She made out her will and wrote goodbye letters to loved ones. Still, when asked later if she was afraid, she coolly responded, "I'm sorry to be a disappointment in answering.... It would sound more exciting if I only could admit having been shockingly frightened. But I honestly wasn't."

Earhart was named captain of the flight and was responsible for making all decisions on board. Bill Stultz was appointed as the pilot, and Slim Gordon accompanied them as the mechanic. On June 17, 1928, the group of three took off from Newfoundland in a plane aptly named *Friendship*. Twenty hours and forty minutes later they landed safely in Burry Port, Wales. When the people of Burry Port saw Earhart step out of the plane, they were overcome with joy. "In the enthusiasm of their greeting, those hospitable Welsh people nearly tore our clothes off," she later reported. Earhart was an instant celebrity and became famous around the world. When she returned to America, a ticker-tape parade was held in her honor in New York City. She met President Calvin Coolidge and other distinguished dignitaries. She could not go anywhere without being besieged for autographs. Due to her courage and an uncanny resemblance to Charles Lindbergh, she was given the nickname, "Lady Lindy."

Earhart was uncomfortable with her newfound fame and thought it was unwarranted. She believed all of the accolades should go to the pilot because she had not handled the controls for even one minute of the flight. As she put it, she was no more helpful than "a sack of potatoes." She continued to give all the credit to the pilots. Still, nobody seemed to care about the details. Earhart was the first woman to cross the Atlantic Ocean in a plane and that was enough to demonstrate her bravery and courage. However, Earhart had integrity and wanted to justly earn such fame and notoriety. She knew she was an excellent pilot and wanted to prove it to the world. She privately told friends, "The next time I fly anywhere, I shall do it alone."

On May 20, 1932, she finally proved her abilities to the world. On a route similar to that taken by the *Friendship* four years earlier, Earhart attempted to fly solo over the Atlantic. This time she intended to fly her single-engine Vega all by herself. She began the flight at 7 p.m., intending to fly throughout the night. However, the plane's altimeter soon failed, making it impossible for her to judge her altitude. Without daylight, she had no idea how close to the ocean she was flying. Making matters worse, she flew directly into a terrible storm. The plane shook uncontrollably in the fierce winds, forcing Earhart to choose between rising above the storm into colder air or diving below the clouds, perilously close to the ocean. Fearful of crashing into the ocean, she chose to fly above the storm. Unfortunately, when she did so, ice began to form on her wings, a dangerous situation that could only be remedied by flying at a lower altitude. Earhart lowered the plane to what she estimated to be a few hundred feet over the ocean's surface. Next, the engine caught on fire, making the situation more hazardous by the minute. Even for a courageous woman, this was a terrifying situation.

Earhart was in the middle of an ocean aboard a burning plane without an altimeter and she could not radio anyone for help. As she later put it, "Probably, if I had been able to see what was happening on the outside during the night, I would have had heart failure then and there; but, as I could not see, I carried on." As day broke over the eastern horizon, she realized all that she was up against. However, she had little choice in the matter—she kept flying and hoping. With less than an hour's worth of fuel, she spotted land. She was aiming for Paris, but found the countryside of Ireland. At that point, it did not matter. Earhart landed safely, becoming the first woman to fly solo across the Atlantic Ocean. Of her landing, she said, "After scaring most of the cows in the neighborhood, I pulled up in a farmer's backyard."

Earhart received even more notoriety than before as the world celebrated her great accomplishment. It was like Neil Armstrong walking on the moon or Michael Jordan hitting a last-second shot to win the NBA Championship. Amelia Earhart was a legitimate hero. She became the first woman ever to receive the Distinguished Flying Cross from the U.S. Congress. Vice President Charles Curtis praised Earhart for her "heroic courage and skill as a navigator at the risk of her life." Her accomplishments were celebrated by all, and she became an inspiring role model for women in particular. Earhart always wanted women to believe in themselves and fight for greater equality. She believed her achievements in the air demonstrated that men and women were equal in "jobs requiring intelligence, coordination, speed, coolness, and willpower."

Her notions of equality in relationships went against the traditional thinking of the day as well. Her first boyfriend proposed marriage, but she was unwilling to give up her career to be a stay-at-home wife and mother. She cherished her independence and knew most men's notions of marriage would not include her flying. Because of her strong beliefs, Earhart declined his proposal. Her next serious suitor was George Palmer (G.P.) Putnam II, a wealthy publisher who quickly fell head over heels for Earhart. From 1930 to 1931 G.P. proposed to her six different times. She said no five times. She was a woman with ambition and dreams. The last thing in the world she wanted was a man to tell her what she could and could not do. G.P. finally convinced her that he did not want to limit her career. In fact, he suggested that he become her manager and promoter. With this understanding, Earhart finally said yes to his sixth proposal. She and G.P. Putnam were married in 1931. Like everything Earhart did, she also had an unconventional approach to marriage. She kept her maiden name professionally, but used her husband's last name in her private life. Unlike most of her contemporaries, Earhart viewed marriage as an equal partnership.

Central to her efforts to bring more women into aviation, Earhart and her female peers formed an organization exclusively for women pilots. The organization was named the Ninety-Nines—the number of charter members who founded the group. Earhart became the group's first president, and under her leadership, the Ninety-Nines sponsored air races and provided financial aid to struggling members. Today this organization has about 6,000 members worldwide and awards the Amelia Earhart Memorial Scholarship each year.

During her lifetime, Earhart traveled around the country speaking about women's rights and encouraging Americans to fly commercially. She knew that flying would become a popular way to travel once people got over their initial fears of safety. To demonstrate just how safe flying had become, she took First Lady Eleanor Roosevelt for an aerial tour of the Washington, D.C., area. Upon landing, Mrs. Roosevelt exclaimed that flying was "fun," and later she even earned a student pilot permit. Several years later, Mrs. Roosevelt played a significant role in ensuring the 332d Fighter Group, otherwise known as the Tuskegee Airmen, became the first black squadron to fight in combat during World War II.

Earhart continued to set aviation records, even surpassing many male pilots. In January 1932, she set a speed record of seventeen hours and seven minutes traveling from the East Coast to the West Coast of the United States. On January 11, 1935, she became the first person to fly from Hawaii to California. Later that year she was the first pilot to fly solo from Los Angeles to Mexico City and from Mexico City to New Jersey. In 1937, she set a speed record for flying from California to Hawaii in fifteen hours and forty-three minutes. Reporters repeatedly asked her why she continued to take such enormous risks. Her response was usually the same: "For the fun of it." She said it so often that she appropriately used the phrase as the title of her second book.

In 1937, when Earhart was thirty-nine, she commented, "I have a feeling that there is just one more good flight left in my system." That good flight was an attempt to fly around the world at the equator, a 29,000-mile trip. This daring feat had never been attempted. Not only was it dangerous, but the trip would require assistance from the U.S. government, a great deal of money, and a lot of luck. President Roosevelt authorized the U.S. Navy to use its vessels to help Earhart navigate a tricky stretch in the Pacific. Her husband managed to raise the necessary funds through private donations. One such donation came from Bernard Baruch, who accompanied his donation with the following statement, "Because I like your everlasting guts!"

Along with her radioman, Fred Noonan, Earhart took off from Miami on June 1, 1937. Heading east, they traveled some 22,000 miles, making scheduled stops along the way for sleep, refueling, and equipment maintenance. On July 2 they took off from Lae and were scheduled to travel some 2,000 miles before making landfall on Howland Island, between Australia and Hawaii. This was the trickiest leg of the trip because Howland Island is only a half-mile wide and 1.5 miles long—a difficult target to find in the vast Pacific Ocean. A U.S. Coast Guard cutter named *Itasca* was responsible for guiding Earhart to this remote island. Specifically, radio communications would be used to direct the plane toward the island, and when Earhart got close enough, the *Itasca* would send up smoke signals. Unfortunately, the 2,000-mile voyage was filled with communication problems. One hour before the plane's fuel was to run out, the *Itasca* received the following radio transmission from Earhart: "We must be on you but cannot see you. Gas is running low. Been unable to reach you by radio.... One-half hour fuel and no landfall." All attempts to determine the plane's position and respond to Earhart's message failed. Approximately one hour later, a final message was received from a desperate-sounding Earhart. "We are on the line of position 157-337.... Will repeat this message...we are running north and south." She was never heard from again.

The search for this American icon was widespread and unprecedented. Over $4 million was spent on the search, which involved 3,000 people, ten ships, and 102 planes. No trace of Earhart or her plane was ever found. The theories about her death are endless, but subsequent searches have failed to uncover the truth. In fact, three separate research teams spent millions of dollars in 2001 to figure out what ultimately happened to Earhart. Each mission came up empty. The mystery remains unsolved.

As she did before each trip, Earhart wrote a letter to her husband that was only to be opened in the event of her death.

It read, "Please know I am quite aware of the hazards. I want to do it because I want to do it. Women must try to do things as men have tried. When they fail, their failure must be but a challenge to others."

Earhart never had regrets. She lived life to the fullest and brought a certain level of intensity that few of us will ever know. While she died far too early, her courage paved the way for women to earn equality with men in the work world and their personal lives. Her progressive ideas about equality—once considered outrageous—are the norm in the twenty-first century. Because of her pioneering spirit, more women became pilots and more Americans took an interest in flying as a way of travel. For all of these reasons, Earhart is one of the great role models of the 20th century.

Amelia Earhart's life should inspire us all to be more courageous. However, it is important to note that you don't have to risk your life to be a courageous person. Courage can be found in the small details of life. According to author Harper Lee, "Real courage is when you know you're licked before you begin, but you begin anyway and you see it through no matter what." Therefore, a person who is afraid to try something new, but does so anyway is courageous; a person who fails the first time, but tries again is courageous; a person who tells the truth regardless of the consequences is courageous. Amelia Earhart left a legacy that challenges us to stand up to our fears and fight for our convictions.

Christopher Reeve

Appreciation

When Christopher Reeve starred as Superman on film, he was the man of steel. Faster than a speeding bullet! More powerful than a locomotive! Able to leap tall buildings in a single bound! He had superhuman strength and his body was indestructible. Superman was Christopher Reeve's first major movie role. Because he went on to play the superhero in four blockbuster movies, the public came to see no distinction between Superman and Reeve himself. When Christopher Reeve walked down the street, he was often mobbed by people who said things like, "Superman, you're my hero!"

Of course, to Christopher Reeve, Superman was just another role he played on the big screen. Acting was his profession and he enjoyed the thrill of playing complex characters. He was in demand as an actor, appearing in thirty-three films and thirty-one plays. In one film, he might play the part of a villain, in the next a hopeless romantic, and in the next a hero who saves the world from nuclear annihilation. Reeve was not an overnight success as an actor, however. He worked hard over many years to hone his craft. While in high school, he often had the starring role in school plays, before moving on to take smaller roles in local theater productions. In 1973 Reeve was accepted to Juilliard, one of the finest performing arts schools in the country. Of two thousand students who auditioned, Reeve was one of twenty invited to enroll. In addition, he was one of only two students selected to participate in an advanced program at Juilliard. The other student was

Robin Williams, who went on to become a famous actor and comedian.

Outside of acting, Reeve was a good student and an outstanding athlete. He excelled at hockey, soccer, baseball, and tennis. As an adult, he maintained an athletic physique and became more of an outdoorsman. He was a talented downhill skier and frequently traveled to popular ski resorts around the world. Sailing became another one of his favorite activities. When not working, he would explore the vast sea in his sailboat. Reeve also earned his pilot's license and bought an airplane. On two separate occasions, he retraced Amelia Earhart's famous voyage by making solo flights across the Atlantic Ocean to Europe. When Reeve was in his thirties, he discovered a new passion—riding horses in jumping competitions. He loved the competition and sense of independence that riding gave him. Reeve truly felt at home while in the saddle. Before a fateful day in 1995, Reeve trained at least five times a week. As a result, he and his trusted horse, Buck, did well in numerous competitions.

At the age of forty-two, Christopher Reeve was enjoying success in his professional and personal life. He was scheduled to play the lead in a new movie called *Kidnapped* and was preparing to undertake his directorial debut in the romantic comedy *Tell Me More*. He had also received his own star on Hollywood's Walk of Fame and had hosted *Saturday Night Live*. His personal life was equally rewarding. He was married to the love of his life, Dana, and she had recently given birth to their son, Will. Reeve also enjoyed solid relationships with his two older children, Matthew and Alexandra. The summer was fast approaching and that meant traveling, family time, and plenty of outdoor activities.

On Memorial Day weekend of 1995, Reeve was scheduled to ride his horse in a competition in Vermont. At the last minute, he changed his mind, deciding to join some friends at another competition in Culpeper, Virginia. The day before the competition, Reeve walked the cross-country course to plan how he would guide his horse through the jumps. The next day, he repeated this ritual to make certain that he was prepared for the competition. Reeve was not worried about the third jump on the course since it was only three feet tall. After plotting his strategy, he returned to the stables and told a friend that he was looking forward to a good ride. Reeve later wrote, "From that moment until I regained consciousness several days later in the intensive care unit at the University of Virginia, I have no memory of what occurred." He did not remember that his horse suddenly stopped just as he was supposed to jump the third gate. He did not remember that his horse bucked, sending him head first into the third gate. He did not remember that his hands got tangled in the bridle, leaving him unable to break his fall. And he did not remember lying on the ground gasping for air as he fought for his life. The mind has a funny way of protecting people from terrible events that dramatically change their lives forever.

Unfortunately, just because Reeve does not remember the fall doesn't mean it did not happen. It did. Reeve landed squarely on his head, and the fall broke his neck. It was the worst kind of neck injury. He shattered his first cervical vertebra (C1) and also broke his second vertebra (C2). The vertebrae are numbered from the base of the neck down the back toward the tailbone, with the lower numbers at the top. In a back or neck injury, the higher the site of the injury, the more severe it is. If an injury occurs at the C5 or C6 level, the victim usually becomes a paraplegic, losing feeling and control below the waist. For Reeve and others who break their C1 vertebra, the impact is more severe. Reeve's injury resulted in no feeling below his neck. The accident left him a quadriplegic, meaning he no longer had the use of his legs or arms. Even worse, he was dependent on a ventilator to help him breathe.

Most people who break their C1 vertebra do not survive. They often die immediately from a lack of oxygen or contract pneumonia shortly after being injured. Soon after arriving in the intensive care unit, doctors took Reeve into surgery to reattach his head to his spinal column. He was given slightly less than a fifty-fifty chance of survival. At one point, he mouthed to his wife, "Maybe we should let me go." She began to cry, but quickly found the words that would save her husband's life. "I want you to know that I'll be with you for the long haul, no matter what. You're still you. And I love you." Reeve found strength in her words and the love of his family. "I knew then and there that she was going to be with me forever," he recalled. "My job would be to learn how to cope with this and not be a burden. I would have to find new ways to be productive again."

How does a quadriplegic learn to cope with such severe injuries and not be a burden? Without the use of his arms and legs, Reeve was unable to do most of the things that able-bodied people take for granted. He could not feed himself, get dressed in the morning, brush his teeth, or go to the bathroom on his own. He was completely dependent on other people to meet his daily needs. Just moving Reeve from his bed to his wheelchair took a concerted effort from a team of nurses and aides. The help of health care professionals proved just as critical after he came home from the rehabilitation center; he required assistance twenty-four hours a day. However, there were some roles that his health care aides could not fulfill. Reeve was not able to hug his children, for example. He needed to sleep in a special bed, which kept him from sleeping in the same bed with his wife. For a man who had been very active and loved to explore the outside world, play sports, and be an active participant in the game of life, it was an almost unbearable situation. Reeve once wrote, "I would say the worst part of it is leaving the physical world—having had to make the transition from participant to observer long before I would have expected."

He spent many days pondering "what if" scenarios. What if he had gone to Vermont instead of Virginia that weekend? What if he had been able to untangle his hands and brace his fall? The biggest "what if" came from a doctor who studied the MRI of Reeve's spinal cord. He told Reeve that if his head had been twisted a mere fraction to the left, he would have been killed instantly. On the other hand, if his head had been twisted a mere fraction to the right, he would have been on his feet in no time.

Without the ability to move, Reeve was tormented by his thoughts. At first he thought, "Oh God, I'm trapped, I'm in prison. I've got a life sentence here. I'm stuck, I'm never going to get out of this." He also had moments of self-blame, thinking "I've ruined my life, and you only get one."

For many people, life without movement below the neck might not seem worth living. However, in his book *Still Me*, Reeve expressed feelings of hope and gratitude. Despite his injury and the resulting limitations, he filled his autobiography with words such as thankful, appreciative, lucky, and fortunate. Few people would have the courage to turn such a tragedy into a second opportunity at life. Reeve would be the first to say that the transition did not happen overnight. After the accident he was initially filled with self-doubt, suffering setbacks only a quadriplegic could fully understand. But Reeve slowly learned that he still had a lot to offer his family and the world. He could be a loving husband to his wife, a nurturing father to his three children, an advocate for other victims of spinal cord injury, and a source of inspiration to millions of people.

As much as possible, Reeve maintained a positive attitude. He learned to appreciate what he could do, instead of complain about what he couldn't do. He could still think. He could imagine. He could hope. He could smile and laugh at a joke. He could tell his family how much he loved them. He learned to enjoy the small things in life, like the smell of freshly baked bread and the pure beauty of a sunrise. It wasn't just his wife's words that pulled him out of his depression. It was the knowledge that his children still needed him. He realized how unfair it would be to give up and give in to self-pity—unfair to himself and to his family. Slowly but surely, he changed his thinking. He found the best way to do that was to concentrate on the needs of others. As Reeve once commented, "You try to behave in the best manner you possibly can, the most loving way you can manage at any given moment.... Thinking that way helped me get past the 'me-me-me'—my body, my problems, my condition, myself." Reeve had the courage to move on and the wisdom to appreciate those who loved him most.

When the world first learned of Reeve's injury, the reaction was shock and disbelief. Most people thought of Christopher

Reeve and Superman as one and the same. And Superman is indestructible, right? The man of steel, right? For many of us, Reeve's accident made us consciously aware that we are all mere mortals. If Reeve, the epitome of health and vitality, can fall victim to such a tragic accident, then it can happen to anyone.

Once past the initial shock, the public responded with love and compassion. Get-well cards and letters began arriving by the thousands, and Reeve received them with gratitude. He got letters from ordinary people all over the world who wanted to offer their support and good wishes. Old friends wrote to extend their condolences, and people with spinal cord injuries wrote to give encouragement. Adoring fans told him how he had changed their life and given them inspiration. Reeve even received a letter from President Bill Clinton. In total, Reeve was the recipient of more than 400,000 letters. They turned out to be the lifeline that he needed to keep going. "I needed support," he said. "I needed something positive."

When Reeve finally left the hospital and entered a rehabilitation center, he had bodyguards posted outside the door of his room. Facility administrators thought that a celebrity needed such protection. But Reeve was not just a celebrity—he was a human being who needed to be in contact with other patients who were also suffering from spinal cord injuries. He began to leave the door to his room open for other patients to drop by and visit. He ventured out in his wheelchair to other rooms. He learned a lot from the other patients. He met one fourteen-year-old boy who had been paralyzed after being flipped on his head by his brother while wrestling, and he met a senior citizen who had fallen off the roof while painting his house. All the stories were equally tragic and life altering. Reeve began to connect with these people. They helped him accept his condition and to think positively about his future. Reeve was also beginning to realize how fortunate he was. He was wealthy and could afford around-the-clock nursing care in his home. Even people with insurance usually have a million-dollar cap for extensive injuries. That might seem like a lot of money, but that amount can be spent in a matter of months by patients with spinal cord injuries. Most quadriplegics spend the rest of their lives in institutions because their insurance does not cover the care that is needed to lead a "normal" life. Reeve became increasingly frustrated and angered by this situation. He decided to do something for patients who were faced with restrictions on their care.

Reeve was not new to helping people. Long before his accident, he was actively involved with the Make-a-Wish Foundation, an organization that grants wishes to terminally ill children. Children often made a request to meet Superman, and Reeve would visit them in the hospital while dressed in his superhero costume. He also served as a volunteer track and field coach for the Special Olympics. He had been involved in many charities, but this time it was different. As a celebrity and a quadriplegic, he was in a position to help thousands of people suffering from spinal cord injuries. Clearly, he had enough of his own problems to worry about, but as he put it, "I had seen too much of their struggles and pain. I couldn't go home, devote my life to myself and my family, and ignore the larger picture."

Reeve was elected as chairman of the board for the American Paralysis Association. The organization's mission statement is simple: "Find a cure." He also established the Christopher Reeve Foundation, which has raised over $40 million to enhance the quality of life for disabled people. Reeve was committed to funding the work of scientists, doctors, and researchers striving to find a cure. He devoted a lot of time to hosting fundraisers and making speeches all over the country. He kept trying to convince politicians to spend more on research. Mike Manganiello, an executive with the Christopher Reeve Foundation, said, "I've never seen a greater lobbyist in my life than Chris. I saw him change people's minds." About a half a million people become paralyzed each year due to a spinal cord injury, costing the government an estimated $8.7 billion a year to care for them. A fraction of that is spent on finding a cure.

In addition to his work with the foundation, Reeve got a second chance in the entertainment industry—this time as a director for the HBO movie *In the Gloaming.* The film was nominated for five Emmy Awards and won four Cable Ace Awards. In 2004, Reeve directed *The Brooke Ellison Story,* the heart-wrenching story of a college student who was struck by a car and became a quadriplegic, yet still graduated *summa cum laude* from Harvard. The real-life Brooke Ellison said, "I knew Chris would be able to tell my story with a sensitivity nobody else could bring."

Reeve admitted that between his physical therapy, fundraising, and directing career, he was busier than he had been before his accident. In the nine years between his accident and his untimely death, he appeared at the Oscars, spoke at the Democratic National Convention, directed two films, wrote two books, and gave numerous speeches all over the world. A writer from *Newsweek* who got a glimpse of Reeve's schedule once commented, "We should all be so disabled." Reeve's intent was to inspire able-bodied people to do more with their lives. As a quadriplegic, he had a different perspective on life, and at times, became frustrated with people who did not take full advantage of the opportunities they had been given. Reeve said, "I get pretty impatient with people who are able-bodied but are somehow paralyzed for other reasons."

Despite all that he had on his plate, Reeve never passed up the chance to spend time with his family. He got up every morning to see his son off to school. He understood the importance of talking and listening to loved ones. After his accident, Reeve came to understand that "being" was better than "doing." It still saddened him that he couldn't play hockey with his son or teach him to ski, but Reeve understood how vitally important he still was to his son's life. He was able to offer his son advice and support as he got older. Sometimes, Reeve said, he and his son sat and talked for hours. Every parent and child should realize the importance of this kind of time spent together.

Every day Reeve made an effort to finish his exercises and his daily business by 5:30 p.m. so that he could spend time with his family. They often watched sporting events on television together or shared the events of their day. Before Reeve drifted off to sleep each night, his wife climbed into his narrow bed to spend a few minutes together. Unfortunately, the special bed was too small for both of them to sleep on, but he was grateful that she could snuggle up to him every night. After the accident, Reeve learned to appreciate the little things in life, and never again took them for granted.

Reeve made it his goal to walk again. He endured hours of physical therapy every day so that when researchers discovered a cure for paralysis, his body would be ready. Many doctors told him it would be impossible to regain the use of his legs. However, Reeve refused to listen to naysayers. "I've just decided I won't listen to the rules," he said with his usual intensity and determination. Defying medical science, some five years after the accident, Reeve's body began to regain some of its function. In a body that was supposed to be numb, he could once again feel pain and differentiate between hot and cold. "To be able to feel just the lightest touch is really a gift," he said joyfully. "The fact is that even if your body doesn't work the way it used to, the heart and the mind and the spirit are not diminished." One of Reeve's doctors, John McDonald, reported that Reeve regained limited movement in his right wrist, fingers, and toes, and before his death was working to regain movement in other areas of his body. Reeve also underwent groundbreaking surgery that allowed him to breathe without a ventilator. At first, he could only manage without the ventilator for a few minutes, but he ultimately worked his way up to several hours.

Unfortunately, Reeve never achieved his goal of walking again. On October 10, 2004, he died of cardiac failure resulting from an infection throughout his body. His wife and family were with him when he died. A private memorial service was attended by over 900 family members, friends, and admirers.

In a moving tribute, entertainment critic Alex Sandell wrote, "It's fitting he played Superman on screen, because in real life, Christopher Reeve was a hero." Actor Michael J. Fox, who suffers from Parkinson's disease, said, "Chris had far greater challenges than I've faced and faced them with a courage, intelligence, and a dignity I can only aspire to. If he could ever have walked, he would have walked over to help someone else get up." Close friend and fellow actor Robin Williams said, "It's hard for me to believe he's gone because he was such a fighter and such a strong personality and soul to begin with." While the world mourned his death, Reeve's spirit lived on. He was an advocate for stem-cell research and urged politicians to fund this groundbreaking area of science. The U.S. Congress is currently considering passage of The Christopher Reeve Paralysis Act of 2004, which would provide $300 million in additional funding to help reverse paralysis.

There are several lessons to be learned from Christopher Reeve. First, life is fragile and can change in an instant. Tomorrow is promised to no one. Therefore, we should take advantage of what life has to offer today and appreciate each and every day. Compared to Reeve's limitations, most of our problems are insignificant, or at least surmountable. Most people get caught up in the little things in life that don't really matter and lose sight of their dreams for the future. In his second book, *Nothing is Impossible*, Reeve wrote, "So many of our dreams at first seem impossible, then they seem improbable, and then, when we summon the will, they soon become inevitable."

We should not wait until a tragedy occurs to recognize all the gifts life has given us. Be thankful for those who love you. Spend time with them and let them know how much they mean to you. Be thankful that you can run, jump, hear, see, and live a healthy and active life. Remember that whatever hand life deals you, do not fold your cards. If you continue to believe in yourself and persevere, something positive will eventually happen. Whether we realize it or not, we are all given opportunities. Take advantage of them.

Another important lesson we learn from Reeve is that it is not enough to take advantage of our own opportunities. We need to seize opportunities to help others who are less fortunate, and we need to abandon the "me-me-me" mentality that is so prevalent today. Ask yourself what you can do to help others. Volunteer in the community, donate to a charity, or send a note to someone who is having a bad day. By helping other people, we begin to recognize the blessings in our own lives.

Before his death, Reeve was asked, "What is a hero?" He responded, "I think a hero is an ordinary individual who finds the strength to persevere and endure in spite of overwhelming obstacles." Using this definition, everyone has the opportunity to be a hero. While most Americans would agree that Christopher Reeve was a hero, we should all recognize him as an outstanding role model who exhibited strong character to millions of people worldwide.

Martin Luther King Jr.

Self-Control

On July 4, 1776, representatives from the original thirteen colonies signed the Declaration of Independence, which laid the foundation for freedom and democracy in what would become the United States of America. The second paragraph of this document clearly states the beliefs of our founding fathers, "We hold these Truths to be self-evident, that all Men are created equal, that they are endowed by their Creator with certain unalienable Rights, that among these are Life, Liberty and the Pursuit of Happiness."

Unfortunately, at the time, these rights only pertained to white men. Slavery was the law of the land, meaning that black people were owned and treated like property. They were viewed as an inferior and uncivilized race and were not granted any of the rights promised in the Declaration of Independence. Slavery began to disappear in the northern states during the early 1800s, but it would require the Civil War (1860–1864) and the signing of the Emancipation Proclamation in 1863 for slaves to be freed in the American South.

While the Civil War ended an ugly chapter in American history, the era of segregation and Jim Crow laws was just beginning. The Civil War freed blacks from slavery, but gaining equal rights took many more decades. For roughly the next 100 years, blacks and whites living in the South had "separate but equal" facilities in public places. Signs saying "White" or "Colored" designated separate drinking fountains, restrooms, barbershops, movie theaters, and other public facilities. This precedent was affirmed in 1896 in Plessy v. Ferguson, when the U.S. Supreme Court upheld a decision finding Homer Plessy guilty of sitting in the whites-only section of a train in Louisiana.

Segregation was snobbery in its ugliest form because it was founded on the misguided premise that whites were the superior race, and blacks were not good enough to sit, be educated, or eat with whites. This separation of the races was a constant reminder that everyone had a place in society and blacks were at the bottom. Separate was not accompanied by equal.

By the middle of the 20th century, black people refused to tolerate this continued attack on their dignity and self-respect. Black individuals had always fought racism in various ways with differing degrees of intensity, but beginning in the 1950s and 1960s they spoke up collectively to fight for equality. This unified voice had a name—the Civil Rights Movement. The leader behind that unified voice was Dr. Martin Luther King Jr. His greatest contribution was recruiting thousands of mostly black individuals to join his nonviolent army and to use the highly effective tactics of sit-ins, marches, and boycotts to gain equality. As a result, civil rights protestors made America a better country for all of its citizens. From the moment he came into the national spotlight in Montgomery, Alabama, in 1954 to the day he was assassinated in 1968, King's strong spirit and charismatic leadership inspired a generation of people to fight for their unalienable rights—the same rights that were guaranteed to all people in the Declaration of Independence.

When Martin Luther King Jr. was born on January 15, 1929, there was no immediate indication that he would change the world. His given name was Michael. When he turned five, his father, also named Michael, changed his own name to Martin Luther, after the founder of the Protestant religion. Young Michael followed suit and thus became known as Martin Luther King Jr. With such a name, it seems he was destined for greatness. His father was pastor of Ebenezer Baptist Church in Atlanta, Georgia, and his mother, Alberta Williams King, stayed home to care for their three children. They were inspiring role models for their son. "I have a marvelous mother and father," King once wrote. "I can hardly remember a time that they ever argued or had any great falling out."

King deeply admired his father, saying, "He is a man of real integrity, deeply committed to moral and ethical principles." As a community leader, Martin Luther King Sr. championed the rights of blacks, working diligently to register black voters and to help black teachers earn the same salary as white teachers. One day a policeman pulled him over for a minor traffic infraction and referred to him as "boy"—one of many demeaning terms white people directed at blacks during that time. Mr. King calmly pointed to his son and said, "That's a boy there. I'm a man." On another occasion, father and son waited patiently at a store to buy shoes. The clerk insisted that they move to the "colored" section of the store before he would agree to assist them. Mr. King said, "We'll either buy shoes sitting here or we won't buy shoes at all." When the clerk refused, King took his son and left the store. Young Martin was learning the ways of the segregated South. He also learned to emulate his father's method of confronting racism with dignity and self-control.

Unfortunately, growing up in the South, Martin had many hard lessons yet to learn. Early in his life, Martin's best friend was a white boy. They often played together when they were very young, but because of segregation they enrolled in separate schools. Soon the neighbor boy told Martin that they could no longer spend time together. Like countless other black mothers of the time, Mrs. King reluctantly sat her son down and explained the concepts of discrimination, prejudice, and segregation. She told him that many white people would perceive him as inferior. More importantly, she ended this talk with a statement she never wanted him to forget: "You are as good as anyone."

In many ways Martin had a normal childhood. He played baseball and football. He loved reading and discovered several black role models through books. Martin was very bright. He skipped several grades in elementary school and was admitted to Booker T. Washington High School, which was named for one of his role models. When he was fourteen, one of his teachers entered him in an educational competition. His speech, "The Negro and the Constitution," won first place. On the way home from the competition, however, he and his teacher sat in the "colored" section of the bus. As the bus filled up, the driver instructed them to give up their seats to a white person. When they didn't move fast enough to suit him, the driver began cursing at them. Martin was forced to bite his tongue, but later recounted, "That night will never leave my memory. It was the angriest I have ever been in my life." As similar experiences accumulated over the years, his contempt toward white people grew.

Martin was accepted to Morehouse College, an all-black school in Atlanta, at the age of fifteen. Even at this tender age, he knew he wanted to dedicate his life to helping others. To earn money for college, he harvested tobacco in Connecticut. During those summers in the North, he was free from Jim Crow laws and enjoyed freedoms he was denied in his hometown of Atlanta. He went to fine restaurants, sat wherever he pleased, and was treated with respect. However, as soon as the train passed Washington, D.C., he was sent back to the "colored" section. After having a taste of what life could be like without segregation, he had trouble adjusting to the loss of freedom, saying, "It did something to my sense of dignity and self-respect."

Partly due to the influence of his father and two of his mentors at college, King decided to enter the ministry. He also understood the powerful influence preachers had in the black community. He was ordained as a minister at the age of eighteen and graduated from Morehouse College the next year. He then enrolled at Crozer Theological Seminary in Pennsylvania. After graduating at the top of his class, he entered Boston University to earn a doctoral degree.

College was an enlightening experience for Martin. It changed the way he viewed the world. He began to interact with white people who empathized with his struggle to overcome racism and shared his desire to end segregation in the South. "As I got to see more of white people...my anger softened," he said. "I began to see that they weren't the enemy. The enemy was segregation itself." Martin also began to encounter philosophers and ideas that influenced his thinking and began shaping him as the future leader of the civil rights movement. He read the work of Henry David Thoreau, who coined the term "civil disobedience." Thoreau wrote, "If a law is unjust, men should refuse to cooperate with it. They should be willing to go to jail for not obeying such a law." He was also heavily influenced by Mahatma Gandhi, who used nonviolent resistance to free India from oppressive British rule. "It was in this Gandhian emphasis on love and nonviolence that I discovered the method for social reform that I had been seeking," he said. He believed that he could help his race overcome racism and segregation by combining Gandhi's nonviolent resistance with Jesus Christ's principles of love and forgiveness.

Martin Luther King Jr. seemed ready for greatness. His parents gave him a solid moral foundation and his education provided him with a remarkable ability to think and reason. He was spiritually grounded and exhibited a calm demeanor, which gave him confidence, even in difficult situations. He had a rare ability to lead people with his actions and inspire them with his words. The final ingredient was added when he married Coretta Scott. King said he knew he wanted to marry her after less than an hour of meaningful conversation. He claimed that she had all the qualities he was looking for in a wife: "character, intelligence, personality, and beauty." They were married in June 1953. King later credited his wife for sustaining him through the tough times that would soon come. "I am convinced that if I had not had a wife with the fortitude, strength, and calmness of Corrie, I could not have withstood the ordeals and tensions surrounding the movement," he said.

After graduating from Boston University, King had several job offers, most of which were in the Northeast. However, he and his wife felt a "moral obligation" to return to the South and try to change the plight of blacks there. King accepted an offer to become minister of Dexter Avenue Baptist Church in Montgomery, Alabama. Montgomery was often considered the heart of the South because it was the most segregated city. From his church, King could actually see the spot where Jefferson Davis took his oath as the President of the Confederate States. Although the Civil War had been over for ninety years, Confederate flags remained clearly visible and the sounds of Dixie could be heard from his church. If King wanted to change things, he had certainly come to the right place.

Not only was it the right place, it was also the right time. In 1954 the Supreme Court ruled on Brown v. Board of Education, declaring that segregated schools were unconstitutional. This decision essentially reversed the Plessy v. Ferguson decision of 1896 and set in motion the wheels of change. On December 1, 1955, a forty-two-year-old black woman named Rosa Parks further challenged the chokehold of segregation by refusing to give up her seat on a city bus. In Montgomery, blacks were expected to sit in the back of the bus and whites sat in the front. On her way home from work one day, Parks sat in the middle—the unreserved section. As the bus filled up with white people, the bus driver directed her to give up her seat for them. When she calmly said, "No," she was arrested for violating segregation laws.

The following morning King received a phone call from E.D. Nixon, who had just posted bond for Rosa Parks and exclaimed, "We have taken this type of thing too long already." Less than twelve hours later, more than forty ministers and civic leaders gathered for a meeting at King's church. The leaders unanimously decided to organize a boycott of the city buses. They handed out thousands of flyers and passed the word through black churches. The following Monday, December 5, the black community responded to the challenge. One empty bus after another passed King's house that morning. Thousands of black individuals walked to and from work, sometimes up to ten miles. King said, "As I watched them, I knew that there is nothing more majestic than the determined courage of individuals willing to suffer and sacrifice for their freedom and dignity."

The boycott was successful, but to have any long-term impact, black citizens knew they needed to organize a long-term effort. The same forty leaders who organized the initial boycott met again later that day. They formed the Montgomery Improvement Association (MIA) and elected twenty-six-year-old Martin Luther King Jr. as their leader. He was surprised to be chosen, because of his age and the fact that he had only been a resident of Montgomery for just over a year. Nonetheless, he was pleased to accept the leadership position. Later that night, the MIA held an open rally. An estimated 5,000 people crowded the church and surrounding streets. King did not disappoint the masses. With only fifteen minutes of preparation and without the use of notes, he gave one of the most inspiring speeches of his life.

> **You know, my friends, there comes a time when people get tired of being trampled over by the iron feet of oppression.... We are not wrong. We are not wrong in what we are doing. If we are wrong, the Supreme Court of this nation is wrong. If we are wrong, the Constitution of the United States is wrong. If we are wrong, God almighty is wrong.... We are going to work together. Right here in Montgomery, when the history books are written in the future, somebody will have to say, "There lived a race of people, a black people...who had the moral courage to stand up for their rights. And thereby they injected a new meaning into the veins of history and civilization."**

That night the world was introduced to Dr. Martin Luther King Jr. through radio and television. And that night the black community unanimously decided to continue their boycott of city transportation until three demands were met: bus drivers would begin treating black passengers with courtesy; passengers would be seated on a first-come, first-served basis; and black bus drivers would be employed on predominantly black routes. For the next 382 days—whether the weather was hot and muggy or cold and rainy—black people refused to ride the city buses.

King viewed the boycott as a nonviolent protest against unjust laws. Years later he wrote in his autobiography, "...What we were really doing was withdrawing our cooperation from an evil system." Of course, many of the white people in Montgomery, including city and state government officials, did not see it that way. They tried everything imaginable to end the boycott and resist changing segregation laws. As King would explain later, "...no one gives up his privileges without strong resistance."

Much of the anger of the city's white leaders was directed at King himself. He was arrested for driving thirty miles per hour in a twenty-five-mile-per-hour zone, the first of thirty times he was arrested during the fight for equality. He received up to forty threatening phone calls per day. One such caller said, "Listen, nigger, we've taken all we want from you; before next week you'll be sorry you ever came to Montgomery." A few nights later, his house was bombed. His wife and first born daughter were in the house at the time, but both survived. Hundreds of black individuals began to form an angry mob outside his house. King kept his composure and addressed the crowd with the following words:

> **We believe in law and order. Don't get panicky.... Don't get your weapons.... We are not advocating violence. We want to love our enemies. I want you to love our enemies. Be good to them. Love them and let them know you love them.... What we are doing is just.**

In the end, his message of self-control won out. On November 13, 1956, the U.S. Supreme Court declared that Alabama's law requiring segregation on buses was unconstitutional. When the order to end this discriminatory policy finally reached Montgomery, the MIA officially ended the protest. King and several of his closest associates were the first blacks to get back on a bus. In a moment that was caught by television cameras and microphones, the bus driver greeted them with a warm smile and said, "We are glad to have you this morning." In a symbolic gesture, King promptly sat down in the front row next to Glen Smiley, a white minister.

The boycott was not just about sitting in the front of the bus; it was about access, equality, and respect. After the boycott ended, King noted the following difference, "The Montgomery Negro had acquired a new sense of somebodiness and self-respect, and had a new determination to achieve freedom and human dignity no matter what the cost." One black janitor also noted the change. "We got our head up now and we won't ever bow down again."

After achieving success in Montgomery, King and his associates formed a church-based organization composed of black ministers from Southern states. King was elected to serve as chairman of the new organization, the Southern Christian Leadership Conference (SCLC). He and his family soon moved to Atlanta to better organize the civil rights movement. As chairman of SCLC, he was responsible for giving speeches across the country and inspiring social change. He was convinced that nonviolent resistance, which included sit-ins, boycotts, and marches, could be a vehicle for change. If it had worked in Montgomery, he thought, it could end segregation everywhere. All it took was courage, cooperation, and large doses of self-control.

Black people all over the South responded to his call. On February 2, 1960, four black students from North Carolina A&T University sat in the white section of a restaurant and ordered coffee. After being denied service, the young men patiently waited at the counter until closing time. The following day, nineteen more black students joined the sit-in. In the following days, more than 100 black students and several white students from the University of North Carolina at Greensboro joined the peaceful protest. Who would have thought it would be such a hassle to get a cup of coffee? Similar sit-ins soon followed in more than 100 cities. Young people, mostly college students calling themselves Freedom Riders, boarded buses in Washington, D.C., and traveled throughout the South. Their main objective was to stop in select cities and use segregated facilities—whites would use "colored" restrooms and blacks would drink from "white" drinking fountains.

Although these began as peaceful demonstrations, they did not always stay that way. The Freedom Riders were routinely beaten with chains, baseball bats, and pipes. When white Southerners heard Freedom Riders were coming to their cities, they showed up in droves. Governor John Patterson of Alabama warned the Freedom Riders to stay out of his state, saying, "Blood's going to flow in the streets."

Other violent incidents were happening with more frequency. Members of the Ku Klux Klan in Mississippi murdered fourteen-year-old Emmitt Till after he allegedly whistled at a white woman. Medgar Evers, a high-ranking member of the NAACP, was shot and killed outside his house in the same state. Four little girls were killed when a bomb exploded at a black church in Alabama. Members of the 101st Airborne Division were called in to supervise the integration of Central High School in Little Rock, Arkansas. Another 20,000 troops were needed at the University of Mississippi when hundreds of white individuals took up arms to deny James Meredith, a black man, entrance to the university.

King was not directly involved in most of these demonstrations. However, he was the glue that kept the movement together. When emotions reached the boiling point, he had the ability to calm the waters. He knew that blacks had the moral high ground and consistently delivered his message of self-control. Nonviolent resistance came from a position of strength, and this strategy enabled the civil rights movement to reach its noble objectives in a just manner. Thousands of people were recruited into King's nonviolent army under the condition that they would not respond to violence with violence. "You must be willing to suffer the anger of the opponent, and yet not return anger," King would say over and over. "You must not become bitter. No matter how emotional your opponents are, you must be calm." It was a hard pill to swallow for many blacks who had dealt with racism all their lives, but by using the strategy of nonviolent resistance, they were making tremendous strides in their quest for equality. The civil rights movement was becoming so successful that King declared, "Old man segregation is on its deathbed."

The only way to put segregation to bed for good was to win important battles in cities like Birmingham, Alabama. The state's outspoken governor, George Wallace, made the following vow in his inaugural address: "Segregation now! Segregation tomorrow, Segregation forever." His racism was only outmatched by Eugene "Bull" Connor, the commissioner of public safety in Birmingham. Together, they governed the most segregated city in America, making it a prime target of King's nonviolent protests.

Because black people had so much buying power, protestors placed most of their emphasis on the business community. They would organize sit-ins, picket local stores, and eventually march on the city until business owners agreed to integrate lunch counters, rest rooms, fitting rooms, and drinking fountains. Hundreds of protesters were arrested every day. King decided to march down to the city courthouse himself. As expected, he was arrested and put in solitary confinement. While in jail, eight white clergy from Birmingham submitted a letter to the local newspaper criticizing the demonstrations. On scrap pieces of paper, King meticulously addressed each of their complaints in his now-famous *Letter from a Birmingham Jail*.

The civil rights crusade continued as thousands of college, high school, and even elementary school students were trained in nonviolent tactics. On the first day of the Children's Crusade, 1,000 marched on the city. On the second day, more than 2,500 followed suit. In response, Commissioner Connor ordered firefighters to shoot powerful streams of water at the children and to release German Shepherd dogs on them. On the third day, the children returned in greater numbers, even more determined to prevail. Connor turned once again to the firefighters and yelled, "Let them have it." At that moment, the children knelt down and began to pray. Apparently mesmerized by the children's courage, the firefighters refused to turn on the hoses. The children politely stood up and marched by them without any further attacks. Birmingham's business leaders soon realized that the movement for equality could not be stopped. They quickly met all of the demands set forth by King. After Birmingham became integrated, it was just a matter of time before Jim Crow was dead and the walls of segregation came tumbling down.

With more confidence than ever before, King led a march on the nation's capital in August of 1963. On the steps of the Lincoln Memorial, overlooking the National Mall, he gave his famous, "I Have a Dream" speech to more than 250,000 people.

> **I say to you today, my friends: so even though we face the difficulties of today and tomorrow, I still have a dream. It is a dream deeply rooted in the American dream. I have a dream that one day this nation will rise up and live out the true meaning of its creed—we hold these truths to be self-evident that all men are created equal.**

King had many dreams. He not only wanted to end segregation, he wanted all people to be treated fairly and equally. He wanted people to be judged by the content of their character and not by the color of their skin. He wanted racial harmony. He wanted to eliminate poverty. At every turn, King fought for these ideals, but in the end his dreams were cut short. In an eerie way, it seemed like he knew before his assassination that he was about to be killed. In his final speech, he said:

> **I just want to do God's will. And He's allowed me to go up to the mountain. And I've looked over. And I've seen the promised land. I may not get there with you. But I want you to know tonight, that we, as a people, will get to the promised land. And so I'm happy tonight. I'm not worried about anything. I'm not fearing any man.**

On the following day, April 4, 1968, King met with his staff to discuss a march that was to be held in Memphis, Tennessee. While on the balcony of his motel, he was shot with a high-powered rifle fired from across the street. The assassin was an escaped convict named James Earl Ray. Dead at the age of thirty-nine, King left behind a wife and four young children. His best friend, the Reverend Ralph Abernathy, conducted the funeral service. Afterward, 50,000 mourners joined the precession to the cemetery. Etched into King's tomb are the following words: "Free at last, free at last, Thank God Almighty, I'm free at last."

Before he died, King said, "If one day you find me sprawled out dead, I do not want you to retaliate with a single act of violence. I urge you to continue protesting with the same dignity and discipline you have shown so far." It would have saddened him to know that more than 100 American cities erupted into violence after his death. Millions of dollars in damages were reported and dozens of black people were killed. The National Guard, once called out to protect black people integrating Southern cities, was now protecting cities from their wrath. But that violence is not King's legacy.

Martin Luther King Jr. was honored many times during his lifetime. In 1963 he became the first black person to be named *Time's* Man of the Year. The following year, he was awarded the Nobel Peace Prize. At the age of thirty-five, he was the youngest person ever to win this prestigious award. Fifteen years after King's death, President Ronald Reagan signed a bill declaring January 15 as a national holiday memorializing Martin Luther King Jr. He is the only American to have a national holiday named exclusively for him.

Now, every year millions of Americans of all races can reflect on King's powerful message of tolerance, equality, and justice. His legacy reminds us what can be accomplished if we work together to overcome our differences. His ability to exercise complete self-control in the face of anger, violence, and hatred is the single greatest factor that enabled him to change so many lives.

We all have a duty to continue King's dream of freedom and equality in America. We must never forget the sacrifices he and thousands of others made to ensure all Americans might enjoy the unalienable rights guaranteed in the Declaration of

Independence. And we must never take these rights for granted. Exercise your right to vote, study hard at the school of your choice, and find a way to contribute to society. Finally, we can honor King by learning to exercise self-control. There are many excuses to get angry, but no good reasons to lose your composure. When we have dignity ourselves and show respect for others, we are honoring the memory of Dr. Martin Luther King Jr.

Helen Keller

Empathy

The Native Americans used to say that empathy was the ability to walk a mile in another person's moccasins. We would now say that empathy is the ability to put yourself in another person's situation and try to understand what he or she might be feeling. This can be done by listening intently to someone's story or by simply imagining the realities of his or her situation. To fully appreciate the life of Helen Keller, you should do both—listen intently and imagine. Imagine what it must be like to go through life without the ability to hear or see anything at all. Close your eyes and plug your ears and imagine what it would be like to try to communicate, to take care of yourself, or to be hopeful about the future. Think of all the sights and sounds that you take for granted as you go through your busy life. As you try to empathize with Helen Keller, be sure not to confuse empathy with sympathy. Sympathy is about feeling sorry for or pitying someone. Empathy is about understanding. Helen Keller would not want your sympathy. She lived a full life, experiencing friendship, love, and loss like anyone else. Unlike most other people, however, she traveled to more than thirty-five countries during her lifetime, meeting kings, queens, and presidents. And perhaps most important, she used her talents to help others who were less fortunate. She would not want your pity, but she would ask for your understanding.

Helen was born in 1880 in the small town of Tuscumbia, Alabama. She had two loving parents, Arthur and Kate; two older half-brothers, James and William; and eventually a younger sister, Mildred. Helen's father was the editor of the local newspaper and a fairly wealthy man. Helen was a healthy baby and enjoyed a normal childhood for the first eighteen months of her life. Like most children, she began walking by her first birthday and could say a few words. One of the words she knew was "water," but it came out sounding like "wah-wah." While visiting her father's prized garden, she could see the colorful berries and flowers, and she could hear the chirping of birds nearby.

When Helen was eighteen months old, she caught a fever. It was an unusually high fever that kept her awake, sweating profusely for days. Without the use of antibiotics, which did not exist at the time, the family's doctor was unable to help Helen and predicted that she would not live. However, her fever finally subsided, and the family was relieved to see her recover. However, they soon began to notice differences in Helen's behavior. She had always had a good appetite and typically responded quickly to the dinner bell, regardless of what she was engaged in doing at the time. After the illness subsided, however, Helen did not seem to notice the bell anymore. Her mother began to wonder about Helen's hearing. As a test, she shook a rattle by Helen's ear. No response. No matter how furiously she shook the rattle, Helen did not respond. Sadly, that was not the only change in Helen's behavior. When the sunlight shone in her eyes, she no longer squinted. Not wanting to believe the worst, her mother began waving her hands and bright lights in front of Helen's face. She did not even blink. The fever had not taken Helen's life, but it had stolen her sight and hearing.

Because the fever occurred before Helen had really learned to talk, she was almost totally devoid of the use of language. She had no way to associate a specific word with a specific object. To her, a pillow was not a pillow. A fork was not a fork. She did not have names for the objects she encountered every day. Without the ability to speak, hear, or see, Helen lived in a world of darkness, something she would later refer to as her "dark and silent world." Over the next few years, Helen developed a few crude gestures to communicate her basic needs. For example, if she wanted her mother, she would stroke the side of her cheek; to ask for a slice of bread, she would mimic a cutting motion. She knew to nod her head up and down for "yes" and shake it left to right for "no." Predictably, Helen became increasingly frustrated when people did not understand her. This led to frequent temper tantrums. Helen later described these tantrums in her autobiography. "I felt as if invisible hands were holding me, and I made frantic efforts to free myself...the spirit of resistance was strong in me." One of the only ways to calm her down was to feed her a piece of candy, but that was only a temporary fix.

During the late nineteenth century, children with disabilities were often branded "idiots" and confined to a mental hospital for the rest of their lives. The Kellers adamantly opposed this approach, but one incident nearly convinced them to institutionalize Helen. When Helen discovered her younger sister sleeping in her favorite crib, she became enraged. She threw one of her famous temper tantrums, this time throwing herself on the crib, which crashed to the ground with the baby in it. Fortunately, the baby was unhurt, but Helen was clearly becoming a danger to herself and others. Her parents did not know what to do and felt they had few options. Raising a deaf-blind child in a normal household was uncharted territory at the time, or so they thought. While searching for some kind of assistance, the Kellers heard about Laura Bridgman, a deaf-blind woman who had learned to communicate through a manual form of sign language. Excited and desperate, Mr. Keller wrote a letter to Michael Anagnos, director of the Perkins Institute for the Blind. In the letter he explained Helen's situation and asked for help. The help came in the form of a fiery, dedicated woman named Annie Sullivan.

It is impossible to tell the story of Helen Keller without also telling the story of Annie Sullivan, the woman known only as "teacher" to Helen. Sullivan knew a few things about overcoming disabilities. When she was only three years old, an infection developed in her left eye. Her family had no money to pay for the necessary treatment. She never fully lost her sight, but her eyes remained tired and weak for the rest of her life. Sullivan's family life was also filled with struggles. Her mother died of tuberculosis and her father was an alcoholic, so Annie and her brother were sent to an orphanage. Her brother soon died in this filthy facility, which was infested with rats and lice. Annie was alone and without hope until someone told her of a special school for the blind—The Perkins Institute. After pleading her case to some compassionate adults, Annie was admitted to Perkins. When she arrived, she could not read or write. At the age of fourteen, she was placed in a kindergarten-level class. She was constantly teased about her perceived lack of intelligence, and she developed a quick temper. In fact, she was almost expelled because of her explosive outbursts and immature behavior. However, a teacher took Annie under her wing and became her role model. Annie began to apply herself and eventually realized her full potential, graduating as valedictorian of her class at Perkins.

Because of Annie's success in overcoming her difficult background, the director of the Perkins Institute recommended her for the job of teaching Helen Keller. It almost seemed like fate that these two strong-willed individuals would come together and eventually form such a strong bond. Of their first meeting, Keller would later write, "The most important day I can remember in all my life is the one on which my teacher, Anne Mansfield Sullivan, came to me."

Like many worthwhile ventures, this teacher-student relationship got off to a rocky beginning. Sullivan arrived at the Keller home in 1887, when Helen was six years old. Sullivan thought Helen's initial appearance was dreadful—her hair was knotted and disheveled, her clothes were dirty and worn. As Sullivan approached her, Helen mistook her for her mother and opened up her arms for a hug. Sullivan obliged the young girl, only to have Helen recoil. One biographer later wrote of this first encounter, "She growled and kicked like a wild animal until the others told Annie to let go."

Sullivan broke the ice by giving Helen a doll, a present from the students at the Perkins Institute. Helen hugged the doll and seemed happy with the present. Her teacher thought this was a good opportunity for Helen's first lesson. She held up Helen's hand, and through the use of manual sign language, she began spelling the word d-o-l-l into Helen's palm. She then placed Helen's hand on the doll. She repeated this pattern many times, hoping that Helen would eventually make the connection between the doll and the word. Sullivan took advantage of every teachable moment. She was constantly spelling new words into Helen's hand. It was difficult work trying to get a deaf-blind child to understand that every object has a corresponding name.

Sullivan believed that Helen was highly intelligent and capable of learning. However, because of her repeated temper tantrums, Sullivan came to the conclusion that Helen needed to be broken—much like a new Army recruit—before she could effectively teach her. Sullivan felt that Helen's parents were a negative influence because they lacked discipline and provided no structure for her. They pitied and spoiled Helen—giving her plenty of sympathy, rather than empathy.

The consequence of their approach was abundantly clear whenever the family sat down for a meal. Helen was in the habit of taking whatever food she wanted from everyone else's plate. She would wander around the table, sniffing each plate and picking up the food she wanted with her bare hands. Sullivan thought this behavior was rude and she intended to put a stop to it. When Helen reached for her teacher's plate, Sullivan slammed her hand down on top of Helen's hand. Wham! Helen was shocked at the response, but would not give up easily. Time after time, Helen tried to take Sullivan's food. Her teacher repeatedly slapped her hand and pinned it to the table. Helen's parents pleaded with Sullivan to just let Helen have her way. However, Sullivan was determined to win this fight. She was intent on teaching Helen a simple lesson in self-control. She suggested that the Kellers wait outside the room. With the door locked and the dining room emptied, the battle of wills ensued. Several hours later, Helen learned to sit at the table, fold a napkin in her lap, and eat with a spoon.

Sullivan knew that as long as Helen's parents continued to give in to her tantrums, she would not be able to teach Helen what she needed to learn. Simple lessons had to be repeated over and over and over for Helen to learn basic concepts. Since the Kellers continued to interrupt the learning process, Sullivan asked to take Helen out of the home for a period of time. The Kellers agreed on the condition that they remain close by. Fortunately, the family had a small cottage on their property that would serve this purpose perfectly. The Kellers rearranged the furniture in the cabin before taking Helen on a long carriage ride. When Helen finally arrived at the cabin, she had no idea the trip had ended several hundred paces from where it began. For all Helen knew, she could have been in another state, or for that matter, on another planet. It was here that Sullivan built the type of relationship that was necessary to teach Helen how to communicate. She cared deeply about Helen and wanted to give her every opportunity to learn. She knew the only way to do this was in a controlled environment where she could repeat lessons every hour of every day. Helen would learn how to function in the world. The cottage became her classroom to learn those basic skills.

Week after week, Sullivan spelled words into Helen's hand. It took time, but Helen began to catch on. She even began to spell the words back into her teacher's hand. It became obvious that Helen enjoyed learning, but she still didn't understand that each object was represented by a specific word. For example, Helen had difficulty understanding that any type of liquid inside a mug had its own unique name (other than m-u-g). One day Sullivan had an idea—an idea that would later be called "the miracle." She took Helen out to a nearby water pump and began pumping water into a mug that Helen was holding. As she always did, Sullivan spelled the word w-a-t-e-r into Helen's hand. Feeling the cold liquid flow over the mug and into her hands, something clicked in Helen's brain. It was the "a-ha" experience of a lifetime. Of this experience, Helen later wrote, "I knew then that w-a-t-e-r meant the wonderful cool something that was flowing over my hand. That living word awakened my soul, gave it light, hope, joy, set it free!" Helen dropped the mug and hurriedly rushed about the property to learn the name of everything she touched. By day's end she knew thirty words, but the most significant moment came when Helen touched her teacher's face, as if to say, "What is your name?" Sullivan spelled out the word t-e-a-c-h-e-r.

On that day, the world opened up to Helen. Just as Sullivan's life was transformed and given meaning by her teacher years before, she passed that gift on to Helen in the same way. In the span of a few months, Helen learned 625 new words. She even learned words to describe the feelings in her heart and the thoughts in her head. Of learning the word t-h-i-n-k, she later wrote, "In a flash I knew that the word was the name of the process that was going on in my head. This was my first conscious perception of an abstract idea." Sullivan also taught her to read Braille, which allowed Helen to explore the world of literature, history, and poetry. Helen loved to learn and eagerly awaited each new lesson. As a result, she soon knew as many words as the average seven-year-old child. This was quite a remarkable feat, considering that she had learned her first word only one year earlier.

Helen's family learned to use manual sign language as well. For the first time, they were able to have a conversation with Helen. Imagine what it must have been like for the Kellers to finally communicate with their beloved daughter. Kate Keller could not contain her emotions when she thought of the transformation in her child. She thanked Sullivan from the bottom of her heart. "I thank God every day of my life for sending you to us, but I never realized until this morning what a blessing you have been to us."

Helen learned to type and soon began writing letters to the director of the Perkins Institute. He published the letters in the school newsletter, along with his comments about her amazing development. Local and national newspapers picked up the story. By the time Helen was eight, she was famous around the world. In fact, the first biography of her was published when Helen was only ten years old. Helen's favorite part of being famous was meeting interesting people and exploring new experiences. She became fast friends with Dr. Alexander Graham Bell, the man who had just recently invented the telephone. Together, they were invited to meet President Grover Cleveland, the first of twelve U.S. presidents whom Helen would meet in her lifetime. She also visited the World's Fair in Chicago. She was granted permission to touch the exhibits, and she learned as much from her sense of touch as other children learned through their eyes and ears. When people wondered how a deaf-blind girl could appreciate art and scenic venues, Helen explained, "The best and most beautiful things in the world cannot be seen or even touched. They must be felt with the heart."

She visited Boston, Niagara Falls, Cape Cod, and New York. She was fortunate enough to learn by doing. She swam and went sailing in the ocean, learned to ride a horse, and slid down snow-covered hills on a toboggan. Helen was experiencing a rich and full life, seemingly without limitations.

Helen had one more educational goal to accomplish. She wanted to attend college. At that time, it seemed unthinkable that a deaf-blind girl would be able to make it through four years of college. But Helen was determined. She would not listen to the naysayers. If there was a way, she was going to make her dream come true. She had her heart set on the best college in the land. Helen told her friends, "Someday I shall go to college—but I shall go to Harvard!" Upon learning that Harvard only accepted male students, she turned her attention to Radcliffe, the sister school of Harvard. Radcliffe had the same rigorous standards as Harvard and offered the same subjects. Students at Harvard and Radcliffe even took the same exams.

To better prepare for college, Helen left the school for the deaf to study at the Cambridge School for Young Ladies in Boston. She had a demanding course load, including classes in German, Latin, French, Greek, and English. She also studied physics, algebra, geometry, astronomy, and history. The only subject she struggled with was math, and she admitted that she had very little aptitude for it. She later wrote, "Arithmetic seems to have been the only study I did not like. From the first I was not interested in the science of numbers."

Helen attended classes with the other Cambridge students, but she could not hear the teacher or see the blackboard. Therefore, Sullivan attended each class with Helen and spelled the lectures into her hand. Afterward, Helen would type up her notes from memory on a special device called a Braillewriter. Sometimes her assigned books were translated into Braille, but other times Sullivan had to read each book and translate it. It was as if Sullivan was attending school too. The two were almost inseparable, studying late into the night. One of the few times they weren't together was during testing periods. Because most people did not understand the language between Helen and her teacher, the school took special precautions to ensure academic integrity. Despite the hardships, Helen passed all of her classes. She would later write of these obstacles, "I have the consolation of knowing that I overcame them all." The director at Cambridge had this to say about Helen's performance: "No candidate in Harvard or Radcliffe was graded higher than Helen for English."

As a result, Helen was accepted to several prominent colleges, but in the end she decided to attend Radcliffe because she wanted to challenge herself. She began college in the fall of 1900 and graduated with honors in the spring of 1904. Of her grand accomplishment, Helen said, "We can do anything we want to do if we stick to it long enough."

Going to college was not something Helen was expected to do, especially in her era. At the time, attending college was the exception, rather than the rule. Helen had already gained respect for her ability to overcome her disabilities and lead a full life. However, she always wanted to push herself. She had an incredible desire to learn, perhaps because she was constantly told what she could not do. To her, it was never good enough to settle or merely get by. She set her sights high and did whatever it took to achieve her dreams. Because of that spirit, she served as a role model for all people with disabilities. She provided hope where there once was none. Many people concluded that if Helen Keller could accomplish so much despite the overwhelming obstacles in her life, others with less significant problems could do the same. To this effect, Keller once wrote, "The most pathetic person in the world is someone who has sight but has no vision." This is a timely reminder that we are all capable of more, provided we give our best effort.

Once Keller reached adulthood, she had no doubt that she would dedicate her life to helping others. As she put it, "Many persons have a wrong idea of what constitutes true happiness. It is not attained through self-gratification, but through fidelity to a worthy purpose." First and foremost, she believed her purpose was making monumental differences in the lives of blind people. Even as a young girl, she began helping others. When Helen was just ten years old, she heard about Tommy Stringer, a five-year-old boy who was also deaf and blind. Tommy lived in an orphanage and was unable to attend school. Helen empathized with Tommy and wanted to help him. She sent numerous letters to wealthy friends asking them to pay for his education at Perkins. The response was overwhelming. Enough money came in to cover the cost of Tommy's tuition. Even as a child, Helen was capable of showing empathy to others less fortunate.

At the turn of the century, blindness was usually due to causes that were entirely preventable. Good medical care was scarce, especially for the poor, who generally had higher levels of illness and disability. Children were especially susceptible to infections that led to blindness. As an advocate for the American Foundation for the Blind for more than forty years, Keller worked tirelessly to educate the public about simple measures that could prevent blindness in young children. She also lobbied the U.S. Congress to begin funding Braille books for the blind. Ultimately, she wanted people with disabilities to have equal access to education.

Keller also became involved in the social issues of her day. In the early 1900s, women were not yet allowed to vote in America. Keller joined the women's suffrage movement, which eventually led to the passage of the 19th Amendment to the Constitution, giving women the right to vote. As a matter of principle, Keller thought it was essential for all citizens to enjoy equal rights in a democratic society. She also had tremendous empathy and respect for working-class Americans. Many of these men and women labored under dangerous conditions, often for very low wages. She wanted to help bring about equality between the "haves" and the "have-nots" of American society. Keller's passion for helping the poor and the uneducated filled her days. In what she called "the crowning experience of my life," she counseled wounded veterans of World War I and World War II. Whether these soldiers came home without legs, arms, eyes, or ears, she gave them hope that they could continue to make valuable contributions to society. "Although the world is full of suffering," she once said, "it is also full of the overcoming of it."

Despite Keller's physical challenges, one of the biggest struggles in her life was with loneliness. She successfully overcame her physical disabilities, graduated from college, and changed the world through her empathic efforts. However, she never fully escaped her "dark and silent life." She once told a dear friend, "I can't imagine a man wanting to marry me. I should think it would seem like marrying a statue." She did have a brief, secret romance with Peter Fagan, who was her secretary for a time. She and Fagan even filed for a marriage license. When Keller's mother found out about the romance, however, she forbade the marriage and kept the two apart. It was a devastating personal loss, but Keller tried to remain optimistic. She often said, "When one door of happiness closes, another opens; but often we look so long at the closed door that we do not see the one that has opened before us."

Although Keller never experienced the joys of marriage, she found happiness behind other doors. She cherished reading and referred to books as her "book-friends." Reading allowed her to escape the physical limitations of her world. Imagination and thought have no boundaries, and Keller loved to learn and explore. Through the ups and downs of her life, Keller had her faithful companion, Annie Sullivan. From the day they met in 1887, they were a team. When Sullivan died in 1936, Keller wrote, "I feel that her being is inseparable from my own, and that the footsteps of my life are in hers. All the best of me belongs to her—there is not a talent, or an inspiration, or a joy in me that was not awakened by her loving touch."

Helen Keller's remarkable life story is known to millions of people. During the 1940s, '50s and '60s, national polls consistently rated Keller as one of the most admired women in America. Numerous biographies were written about her life. One of those biographers was Dorothy Herrmann, who had this to say about Keller: "She was so famous that everyone in the entire world knew who she was and followed her career with avid interest, not only ordinary people, but kings and queens and presidents." British statesman Winston Churchill once called her "the greatest woman of our age."

At different periods in Keller's life, Hollywood approached her with proposals to tell her life story on the big screen. The first movie made about Keller's life was a silent film produced in 1918. Her story was also featured in a documentary, *The Unconquered*, which won an Academy Award in 1954. In 1959, the play *The Miracle Worker*, a tribute to Annie Sullivan's heroic efforts to educate Helen Keller, opened on Broadway. It won the Pulitzer Prize. When it was made into a film in 1962, the actors who played the roles of Helen and Annie won Academy Awards for their performances. *The Miracle Worker* has become a classic and was remade in 1979 and 2000. Throughout her lifetime, Keller gave speeches around the world to great acclaim. In 1964, four years before her death, Keller received America's highest civilian honor when President Lyndon Johnson awarded her the Presidential Medal of Honor. America owed Keller a debt of gratitude for all she did to help others.

Keller wrote about the early years of her life in her autobiography, *The Story of My Life*, which was first published in 1904. The book was enormously popular and was translated into more than fifty languages. Over the last century, millions of people around the world have read Keller's autobiography. Unfortunately, since her death in 1968, the book has become less popular. What once was common reading in middle and high school has been placed on the back shelves of libraries. According to a recent article, eighth-grade students are now more likely to know a joke about Helen Keller than to know that she wrote a highly acclaimed book. That is a shame, particularly because she wrote a thirteen well-received books in her lifetime. "If all you know are stupid jokes about Helen Keller," says educator Carol Jago, "you're missing the whole richness of what other people share and understand about what this woman achieved."

It is important to bring the story of Helen Keller back into the consciousness of America's youth. Her life, marked by hardship, perseverance, and kindness, should inspire empathy for those whom we regard as different or less fortunate. Even if we haven't stood in someone else's shoes, we can listen and imagine.

Bob Hope

Gratitude

Bob Hope lived to be 100 years old, a milestone that few people reach. His life reads like a history lesson. He experienced firsthand many noteworthy events of the 20th century. For example, during his life he witnessed major advancements in transportation, from the automobile to the airplane to the space program. When he was a child, radio was still a new-fangled form of entertainment, but Hope later saw the birth of cinema, television, and the Internet. He lived through the Great Depression, five wars, and countless world tragedies. Through it all, Bob Hope was one of the most beloved and celebrated entertainers of the 20th century. He made seventy-five films, took part in 475 television programs, and wrote ten books in his 100 years of living. However, he is most noted for entertaining U.S. military troops during every war from 1941 to 1990. Over and over again, he said thank you to those brave men and women who fought for freedom and democracy.

Bob Hope was born on May 29, 1903, in England. When Bob was four years old, his family came to America through Ellis Island and settled in Cleveland, Ohio. With seven boys, the Hope family didn't have much money, but they laughed often and humor got them through the tough times. "One of my memories was [my mother's] Saturday night routine," Hope fondly recalled. "She'd get out a big washtub and give us baths in the kitchen." Baths were given in order of how well behaved the Hope boys had been all week. "If we'd been good, we got fresh water," explained Hope. It was one of his first lessons in the benefits of exhibiting good character.

Hope decided to forgo college and pursue his dream of becoming an entertainer. He knew he did not want a conventional job, but in those early days, there were many times when he couldn't afford rent and often went hungry. In those lean times, his mother was his biggest supporter and often wrote him letters urging him to keep going. "One of the greatest things about my mother was that she never stopped encouraging us," said Hope.

Hope entered show business in 1924 as a song and dance man, but it was his quick wit and unstoppable sense of humor that eventually made him famous. Early in his career, he traveled endlessly from one city to the next playing the local vaudeville theaters, where he entertained large and small audiences alike. Hope was one of more than 20,000 vaudeville performers in the 1920s, but he easily transitioned to radio, the next hot fad. He created and produced one of the most successful weekly radio shows of the 1930s and '40s.

Hope went on to conquer the movie industry, as well as the newest invention entering America's living rooms—the television. During his first televised show, Hope joked about this new medium. "For years I've been on radio. You remember radio—blind television?" He worked hard between 1924 and 1941 to build a lucrative career in show business. Hope went on to be a part of every major media form created in the 20th century. Very few entertainers, if any, can make that claim.

Hope worked hard to achieve the American dream, but he felt a need to give something back, too. He began his fifty-year relationship with U.S. military troops in 1941 by broadcasting his hit radio show from military bases. At first, he was innocently looking for a large audience on which to test his material. Performing for 2,000 entertainment-hungry GIs was the perfect setting. Soon, however, it was about much more than just testing his material. Hope liked the idea of entertaining GIs who were fighting to preserve the American way of life he had grown to enjoy. He began a lifelong commitment to the troops when he partnered with the USO (United Services Organization) and began traveling around the world to bring a piece of home to the troops.

The mission of the USO was "to provide morale, welfare, and recreation-type services to our men and women in uniform." No one fulfilled this mission better than Bob Hope. He would gather up the best musicians, singers, and actors to produce a show, rehearse it, and take it on the road to military bases, camps, and hospitals wherever GIs were stationed. "When I saw Bob Hope I was probably as homesick as any one person could be," said one Air Force serviceman, "but he brought a bit of America and home to each one of us, and after that, life was much easier." Over the years, Hope headlined approximately sixty tours including those during World War II, the Korean War, Vietnam, and the Persian Gulf War.

Hope encouraged and supported servicemen and women, often in perilous times, simply because he knew that taking their minds off their situation for an hour or two was the most valuable thing he could do. He thought of them as family. Just as humor got the Hope family through tough times when they didn't have much, Hope's humor would also get the troops through their own tough times. "The Hopes of Eltham, England, and Cleveland, Ohio, had a clannish instinct," he recalled. "We stuck together.... I know it works the same way with men in the same army or marine outfit...."

His first tour took him to military bases in Alaska, where soldiers were located in a desolate area and in desperate need of a morale booster. "Some of these boys have been stuck out in a godforsaken outpost for more than a year—with old books, old newspapers, old movies, and stale relationships. I don't think you have any idea what you're doing for them," said Army General Simon Buckner. Hope and his cast of entertainers performed several shows in the remote corners of Alaska, and that first trip changed him forever. He was touched by what the soldiers endured and was grateful for the sacrifices they were making. It was the first of many trips to come.

In 1943 Hope led a group of entertainers on the first overseas USO trip. The tour took them to bases in Africa, Sicily,

Bob Hope and Frances Langford perform for the troops in World War II.
Photo courtesy of the Dwight Eisenhower Presidential Library [69-229-5].

and Iceland, as well as into the war zones of England. The realities of war were all around them as air raids and bombs came dangerously close. "It isn't often that a bomb falls so close that you can hear it whistle," wrote WWII journalist Ernie Pyle. "The Hope troupe can now describe that ghastly sound." Hope later said that the only thing that went through his mind during those brushes with death was the thought of his wife waiting for him at home. "I've had a number of close calls," recalled Hope of traveling with the USO. "When I remember them I get an uneasy feeling that I'm living on borrowed time. Especially when I recall the close calls I had flying a million miles or so for the USO in WWII."

Hope's commitment to the troops was so strong though that nothing could make him pack up and return home, not even bombs falling a little too close for comfort. He continued performing at camps and visiting the wounded at numerous hospitals. "There isn't a hospital ward that he hasn't dropped into and given a show; there isn't a small unit anywhere that isn't either talking about his jokes or anticipating them," commented actor Burgess Meredith. "What a gift laughter is! Hope proves it."

Hope often said that performing for the troops provided him with the most memorable experiences of his life. "I wouldn't trade it for my entire career," he said. "Until you've actually seen them in action, you have no conception of their courage." Hope was courageous too, and he proved it by continuing to tour time and again. In 1944 he went to the South Pacific, and in 1945 he traveled to France, Germany, and England. In Nuremberg he did a show for 20,000 GIs and stayed in a hotel with only three walls—the fourth had been destroyed by bombs. When he returned from these trips he often spent hours calling GIs' loved ones and passing on messages from GIs he met. It was important to these servicemen and women that their loved ones knew they were okay. Hope unselfishly took the time to personally deliver each message.

Loved ones left to worry on the home front also motivated Hope to continue traveling abroad to military bases. When people asked him why he went on so many trips, he often talked about the father of one particular GI. "He stopped me in a hotel lobby and asked me how his boy had looked when I'd seen him in Kwajalein. We both knew there were five thousand fellows there that day," said Hope. "But it made him feel closer to his son to know that we'd been under the same patch of sky—for a moment."

While Hope was traveling to entertain the troops, often for weeks at a time, he was also leaving his own family behind. His wife, Dolores, was a singer, and they adopted a little girl named Linda, the first of four children. Hope loved fatherhood. "Once we got her home, I was enthusiastic about the whole business," said Hope. "Everything began to revolve around her, and she wound herself around me like a small blonde boa constrictor." Bob and Dolores adopted a son, Tony, a year later. They wanted to continue to add to their family, but Hope was away during WWII entertaining the troops so frequently that they put more adoptions on hold for six years. When he returned in 1946, they visited the adoption agency again. To their surprise, a little girl and a little boy were both available for adoption. Bob left Dolores alone in the nursery to decide which child she wanted to take home, while he went to the office to talk with the administrator. "When Dolores came in a little later, still puzzled about what decision to make, I'd already signed for both babies," recalled Hope.

In addition to the sixty tours he did for the USO, Hope spent much of his time acting, writing, and appearing at countless charity events. Needless to say, he was away from home quite a bit even during peacetime. Married to Dolores for seventy years, she was the glue that held the Hope family together. "Dolores has a wise and loving touch with our children," said Hope. "I'm lost in admiration of the job she has done with them and with the job she's done keeping me in line." His oldest daughter, Linda, understood that her father had numerous commitments, and was grateful for the time they could share as a family. "I think we missed him a lot when we were growing up. The thing about him was that when he was there, the quality of time was so terrific that it did make you miss him when he wasn't there," she recalled.

Hope sacrificed holiday celebrations with his own family to begin what became his annual Christmas tour to visit the troops. Beginning in 1957 his Christmas tour was turned into a popular television broadcast. These shows brought the sacrifice of the American GI to Americans at home. "The American television audience could see that Bob had gone to faraway places, had endured the same unpredictable weather and hardship conditions the GIs were subjected to, and had brought them a laugh and a touch of home," said one biographer.

Producing these Christmas shows was expensive. They often went over budget, but Hope personally covered the extra cost because he believed so strongly in what he was doing. He made the choice to forfeit his family holidays because he knew that the U.S. soldiers were making a bigger sacrifice. Those men and women had no choice, particularly during WWII, Korea, and

Vietnam, when the draft was still in place. They couldn't put down their guns, cease fighting, and travel home for the holidays. Hope, however, had a choice. Congressman Paul Findley said, "Christmas away from home, whether in the cold reaches of Germany during WWII, or the sweltering heat of Vietnam years later, was still enjoyable and memorable to millions of American men and women because Bob Hope was there."

During the Vietnam War, Hope faced new challenges. Vietnam was the first military conflict to be broadcast into American homes on the evening news, and there was a strong anti-war culture among America's youth. Hope took his USO tour to Vietnam nine times between 1964 and 1972, and in a book about his 1964–65 tours of Southeast Asia, he wrote, "I might as well admit it, I have no politics where the boys are concerned. I only know they're over there doing a job that has to be done, and whatever is best for them is best for me." He supported the troops first and foremost. "We might be fighting an unpopular war, but we have five or six thousand of the most popular Americans I know fighting like crazy to preserve our way of life," he said. Although the Vietnam War was very different from WWII, the soldiers fighting in both had the same basic needs. They were far from home and fighting in a foreign land. And after each trip, Hope continued to bring their personal messages home to share with their families.

During one of his Christmas tours in Vietnam, Hope reached Saigon to find that a nearby hotel had been bombed moments before his arrival. He and his cast of entertainers ignored the dangerous conditions and checked into another hotel nearby. Hope immediately went to the Naval Medical Corps facility to visit the injured in the burn ward. "Burn wards are the toughest of all...you wonder if your stomach will allow you to continue," he once said. Hope came across one marine whose injuries were being examined by a doctor. "He looked up at me, his face covered with blood, and said 'Merry Christmas' as if he really meant it, and I don't suppose I will ever forget the way he said it. It still chills me," recalled Hope. He visited hospitals on all his tours before and after the shows. It was difficult not to get depressed or jaded by the horrific sites he encountered, and even more difficult to go out on stage and be funny for an hour or two after these visits. But those experiences only made Hope work harder because he knew that many soldiers would pay the ultimate price in their fight for democracy and would not make it home. Those moments of ease filled with laughter would be the last for many of them.

Each of Hope's shows was unique. Surprise guests, including some of the most beautiful actresses of the day, often joined him on stage. The shows were a combination of comedy, musical performances, and crowd participation. Hope usually brought down the house with his jokes and impeccable timing. An entire room still holds the 85,000 jokes that he told at one time or another. He kept his material fresh and was not afraid to poke fun at the current situation. During a tour in Vietnam, he joked, "I have good news for you guys, the country is behind you fifty percent." The servicemen in the audience smiled, laughed, clapped, and cried at some point during every show. One of the classic songs he performed near the end of the show was *Thanks for the Memories*. Hope wanted every GI to know how honored he was to entertain them.

After the Vietnam War ended, Hope continued to visit military hospitals. From 1973 through 1975, he made it a priority. "For most of us, the war is over. For many of these kids it will never end," he said. Many soldiers sustained injuries during the Vietnam War that would leave them debilitated for the rest of their lives. As Hope went from bed to bed, many of the wounded soldiers would share stories of where they were stationed overseas and at what base they saw his show. He would reminisce with them as if they were old friends. He also continued to travel to bases around the world and to put on his show even in peacetime.

Remarkably, in 1990, when Hope was eighty-seven years old, he packed his bags and gathered a group of entertainers for his last big overseas show and what would also be his last Christmas show. Hope headed to Saudi Arabia, where the Persian Gulf War

At the 1995 Bob Hope Classic, a vibrant ninety-two-year-old Bob Hope plays golf with Presidents Bill Clinton (center), George H. W. Bush, Gerald Ford and past champion, Scott Hoch. Photo courtesy of the William J. Clinton Presidential Library [P24585-16a].

and Operation Desert Storm were in full swing. Security was much more intense than it had been in the past; even Hope's jokes were screened by the State Department. The tour was a success despite the close scrutiny, and for one final time, the world-famous comedian was able to bring the men and women of the Armed Forces some much needed entertainment during the holidays.

For all his commitment, Americans love Bob Hope. There is a warehouse in California that houses the many awards he won during his lifetime. In 1962 President John F. Kennedy presented Bob Hope with the Congressional Medal of Honor, the highest recognition offered to a civilian. The president said it represented "the great appreciation we have for you for so many years of going so many places to entertain our sons, daughters, brothers, and sisters of America who were so very far from home." Hope, as always, responded with humor. "There is one sobering thought: I received this for going out of the country. I think they're trying to tell me something," he said. Little did everyone know that he would continue to entertain the troops for almost thirty more years.

In 1997, an Act of Congress made way for Hope to receive his most valued honor: he was made an honorary veteran of the U.S. Armed Forces. He cried when the resolution was read, and Dolores spoke for him when she said, "I've been given so many awards in my lifetime, but to be numbered among the men and women I admire most is the greatest honor I have ever received." President Bill Clinton then signed the bill into law and Hope went on to visit the Vietnam War memorial. He stood alone for a long time as he looked over the wall that held the names of so many of the soldiers he had seen in the audiences during his nine trips to Vietnam. Each of the 58,245 names on that wall represented a life that was lost as American soldiers fought to protect freedom and democracy. Hope was so grateful for those sacrifices, none of which could ever be repaid, that he made it his lifelong duty to prove just how thankful and appreciative he was. But all those servicemen and women that Hope reached out to were grateful to him too. He gave them a touch of home and a reminder of the life they left behind, and for many it was their last.

Bob Hope died on July 27, 2003. He was 100 years old. Several city streets, schools, and hospitals across America are named after him. There is a C-17 Air Force plane named *The Spirit of Bob Hope* and a naval ship that bears the name *USNS Bob Hope*. He has had countless awards named after him that are given to those who emulate his good cheer and generous spirit. The Spirit of Bob Hope Award is presented by the USO to "entertainers and other distinguished Americans whose patriotism and service to the troops through the USO reflect that of Bob Hope." The Bob Hope Humanitarian Award was established in 2002 and is presented annually by the Academy of

Television Arts and Sciences. It is one of the highest honors presented by the Academy and is given in recognition of "...his many humanitarian efforts over a long and fulfilling career." Oprah Winfrey and Bill Cosby are past recipients.

All of these honors and heartfelt tributes recognize what Hope unselfishly gave American troops for over fifty years. It is not uncommon to hear stories about how three generations within a family saw him perform. Typically, the grandfather saw him in WWII when he was a young boy; the father saw Hope in Vietnam during a much different war; and the son saw him during the Persian Gulf War in yet another far-off corner of the world. One member of the U.S. Army, who was the son and grandson of veterans who had also seen Hope perform, captured the essence of Hope's greatest gift and expressed his gratitude by saying, "For three generations you have braved hostile environments to entertain your boys, the troops. In doing so you did more than just entertain, you gave us your name, you gave us Hope." Thank you, Bob Hope.

Arthur Ashe

Tolerance

When ESPN counted down the top 100 athletes of the 20th century, eight tennis players made the list. Yet the name of Arthur Ashe, who won several tennis championships in the 1960s and 1970s, was nowhere to be found. This was not necessarily an error in judgment or an oversight by the selection committee. Ashe was undoubtedly considered for the list, but the athletes were judged solely on their on-court performances, not what they did off the court. If the selection criteria had included character and off-the-court accomplishments, the outcome would have been far different. As ESPN commentator Dick Schaap put it, "[Arthur Ashe] was a very, very, very good tennis player, but he was not one of the two or three greatest tennis players of all time. But if you voted on the two or three most impressive, most significant athletes of all time, you would put Arthur Ashe up there with Jackie Robinson and Muhammad Ali." Ashe was indeed a great tennis player—at one point in his career he was ranked number one in the world—but he was unquestionably a better person than he was an athlete.

In 1993 ESPN, the same organization that did not include Ashe in its list of the century's top 100 athletes, created the ESPY Awards to recognize top achievements in sports. The most prestigious part of this event is an award that is presented annually to an individual whose contributions transcend sports. This award is appropriately named the Arthur Ashe Courage Award to commemorate Ashe's role as a humanitarian and a champion of important causes. The first person to win this esteemed award was Jim Valvano, the famed former basketball coach at North Carolina State University, who was dying of cancer at the time. It was during his acceptance speech that he included the now famous phrase, "Don't give up. Don't ever give up!" Other notable winners of the award include Muhammad Ali (1997), Pat Tillman (2003), and four passengers from United Airlines Flight 93, who valiantly attempted to regain control of a plane hijacked by terrorists on September 11, 2001. These individuals and the other recipients are recognized as heroes and role models. Yet the award is named for a quiet, skinny tennis player who is generally not ranked among the world's best athletes. Why did ESPN believe Ashe should be the one person so closely associated with this award? What did he do to set himself apart from all the other athletes who came before him?

To properly answer this question, one must start at the beginning. Arthur Ashe was born in 1943 and was raised in Richmond, Virginia, by a loving mother and a demanding father. Arthur's first major setback in life occurred just before he turned seven years old, when his mother died suddenly. He had few clear memories of his mother as he got older, but the feelings of love and the connection he had with her remained intensely present throughout his life. His father took on the role of sole provider for Arthur and his brother. Once a journalist asked Ashe, "How is it that I have never heard anyone say anything bad about you?" Typical of someone raised in his generation, he said, "I guess I have never misbehaved because I'm afraid that if I did anything like that, my father would come straight up from Virginia, find me where I happen to be, and kick my ass." Of course his gentlemanly behavior was driven by much more than a healthy fear of his father. Each Christmas, he and his father delivered food and toys to needy families. The act of giving away brand-new toys each year helped Arthur understand the true meaning of Christmas and built the foundation for his compassionate nature.

Ashe said he also felt that his mother was always watching over him and he never wanted to do anything to disappoint her.

He was a religious person and considered the moral implications of his everyday behavior. He spent many hours reading the Bible and discerning the lessons he could apply to his own life. Though Ashe was introspective and a deep thinker, he thought the teachings of the church boiled down to the Golden Rule: Do unto others as you would have others do unto you. Ashe diligently applied this rule to his dealings with other people, although many did not respond to him in the same way.

Ashe's home state of Virginia, like most Southern states at the time, was racially segregated. As a black child, Arthur was not allowed to go to school with or play tennis with white children. He knew that applying to the leading university in his home state, the University of Virginia, was a waste of his time because it too was segregated—for whites only. Segregation was legally sanctioned and permeated every aspect of daily life. Blacks and whites could not eat together in restaurants, ride together on the bus, or use the same water fountains or bathrooms. While all of these restrictions were insulting, the one that bothered Arthur the most was not being able to compete against white tennis players, who were usually the most talented players at the time. Despite not being able to play in youth tournaments, Arthur's game progressed quickly and he was awarded a tennis scholarship to the University of California at Los Angeles (UCLA).

Ashe's introduction to tennis had come at a young age. His dad worked for the Department of Recreation for the city of Richmond, and Arthur spent time with his father at the municipal parks after school. One day he sat and watched Ron Charity, the best black tennis player in Richmond, practice his serve. Suddenly Charity walked over to Arthur and asked, "Would you like to learn to play?" Arthur replied that he would. With that innocent exchange, Arthur took up the game of tennis. Without that particular sequence of events and the kind gesture of just one person, it's possible that the world would not be familiar with the name Arthur Ashe. This incident illustrates an important lesson—life-changing moments happen when we least expect them, and we should be ready to take advantage of them when

Arthur Ashe playing tennis at Forest Hills, N.Y. in 1964. Photo courtesy of the Library of Congress, Prints and Photographs Division [LC-USZ62-116344].

they occur. As fate would have it, Arthur's skill on the tennis court quickly became evident, and Charity became his unofficial coach throughout the remainder of his adolescence.

While playing tennis at UCLA, Ashe won the NCAA singles championship and led his team to the national championship in 1965. During this time, he was asked to play on the U.S. Davis Cup team, a high honor for any tennis player, let alone a collegiate athlete. The Davis Cup is a competition that pits countries against each other to determine an eventual team champion. The United States usually fields a competitive team and is considered a perennial favorite. Ashe was the first African American ever selected for the U.S. Davis Cup team. While this was a milestone for Ashe and all African Americans, it was only one of many firsts that he would experience in his lifetime.

It is fair to say that Arthur Ashe was the Jackie Robinson of tennis. As most people know, Robinson broke the color barrier in baseball and went on to be one of the finest athletes to ever play the game, regardless of skin color. He routinely exhibited grace under pressure and changed the way black athletes were perceived in America. The same could be said of Ashe. Both men exhibited a high level of integrity and broke down many barriers for African Americans in their respective sports.

Like golf, tennis has four tournaments that are considered Grand Slam Events. Winning one of these events is enough to immortalize any player. In 1968, Ashe won the U.S. Open while he was still an amateur. Because he was a college student and not a professional tennis player, he was not allowed to accept the prize money. However, he won a place in history as the first black male to ever win the U.S. Open. In 1970, he won his second Grand Slam event, the Australian Open, again becoming the first African American to win this tournament. Five years later he won the most prized award in tennis, the Wimbledon championship. Ashe won the Wimbledon tournament, which is held annually in England, as a ten to one underdog to Jimmy Connors, whose name was later included on the list of the top 100 greatest athletes of the century. Ashe did not win the singles title at the French Open, the fourth grand slam event, but he did win the doubles championship. No black male has won a Grand Slam event since.

In his ten years as a pro, Ashe won fifty-one tournaments, including thirty-three singles titles and eighteen doubles titles. Ashe was especially pleased with his Davis Cup record. He considered himself a true patriot and loved playing for the United States of America. He played thirty-two matches against the best players in the world and won twenty-seven, the most ever won by any individual until that point. He was also appointed Davis Cup captain, amassing a 13-3 record and winning back-to-back titles in 1981 and 1982. By anybody's account, Ashe was a tremendous tennis player, and as such, was inducted into the Tennis Hall of Fame for his athletic achievements. However, he was more proud of his demeanor on the court than his actual accomplishments, saying, "I had done nothing, through scandal or bad behavior, to bring the game into disrepute."

It was always important to Ashe to be a leader on and off the court and to display outstanding character. He wrote in his autobiography, "I want to be seen as fair and honest, trustworthy, kind, calm, and polite. I want no stain on my character, no blemish on my reputation. I know that I haven't always lived without error or sin, but I also know that I have tried hard to be honest and good at all times." These are not the usual sentiments we hear from professional athletes. From an early age Ashe wanted to be a decent person and to treat others with civility. More than that, he recognized injustice in the world and fought hard to remedy it.

One reason he felt so strongly about inequality was his memory of the discrimination he experienced early in life. He did not want others to face such hatred. And though Ashe had a special place in his heart for his own race, he wasn't merely concerned with the plight of African Americans. He wrote, "In the end, I am not for black or white, nor even for the United States of America, but for the whole of humanity. I can't define myself finally as an African American, or American. My humanity comes first." That statement, more than any other, is the essence of Arthur Ashe. He had compassion for, and was tolerant of, all people. Whenever and wherever he saw injustice, he was determined to do something about it.

Once Ashe became a prominent athlete, he used his status to become a social activist. He later reflected, "I wanted to make a difference, however small, in the world, and I wanted to do so in a useful and honorable way." After Ashe won the U.S. Open in 1968, a white South African player told him that he would not be allowed to play in an upcoming tournament in Johannesburg. South Africa at the time was operating under the rule of apartheid, which legalized racial discrimination by the white English/Dutch colonialists against the black Africans. Under South African law, Ashe was not allowed to play in a tournament against white players, despite proving that he could compete with and beat many of these players. This ruling was reminiscent of Ashe's younger days in Virginia, and he was not about to let this form of discrimination continue without a fight. When Ashe applied for a visa to enter South Africa in 1969, his application was rejected. He applied again in 1970, 1971, and

1972. Rejected, rejected, rejected. Finally, his application to enter the country and play in the South African Open was accepted in 1973.

Ashe played well in his matches, winning the doubles championship and finishing second in the singles event. However, his real goal was to learn more about apartheid and create change. Before agreeing to play, he demanded that seating for his matches be integrated, a request that was granted. Before and after his matches, he went out to meet with the people and see for himself the injustices that were occurring in South Africa. Black people were not allowed to vote in their own country; whites and blacks were not allowed to marry each other; blacks were assigned to limited regions of the country in which they could live and were required to carry passbooks in order to enter white areas. This practice essentially kept blacks from moving about freely within their own country. If blacks refused to carry a passbook or protested against this immoral form of government, they could suffer strict penalties.

As an American, Ashe was permitted to move freely around South Africa, and as you might imagine, this created quite a stir. One black child followed him every day and curiously watched his every move. Ashe finally approached the boy and asked, "Why are you following me around?" The boy replied, "Because you are the first one I have ever seen. You are the first truly free black man I have ever seen." These words had a lasting impact on Ashe. Armed with firsthand knowledge of this oppressive government and seeing the effects it had on nineteen million blacks in South Africa, he felt an obligation to do more.

Ashe participated in peaceful protests against apartheid, once even getting arrested during a demonstration in Washington, D.C. He also played a major role in getting South Africa banned from Davis Cup play. He called on some of his closest friends to boycott playing in tournaments in South Africa. Ashe made speeches and spoke out against the South African government. He became so involved in protesting apartheid that many people said it interfered with his tennis game. In fact, Ashe only won one Grand Slam Event after 1970. However, he admitted that he was more concerned with freeing millions of oppressed people than simply winning a tennis match, saying, "We must forget ourselves and work for others, even if what we do today may or may not bear fruit until two or three generations." Ashe understood that his role as a human being was to help others, not to serve his own self-interest.

Fortunately, the efforts of Ashe and others did not take two or three generations to create change. Frank Deford, a writer for *Sports Illustrated*, credited Ashe with helping to end apartheid, saying, "Arthur cracked the curtain of apartheid. Once the curtain was opened just a little bit, there wasn't any way the South Africans could bring it back again." In 1977, the United Nations began to put pressure on South Africa to end apartheid. The UN's embargos, sanctions, and boycotts took their toll on the South African government, culminating in an all-race election in 1994. The winner was Nelson Mandela, a black man who had been imprisoned from 1962-1990 for opposing apartheid and the South African government. While in prison, Mandela had read *A Hard Road to Glory*, a three-volume work on the history of African Americans in sports, written by Ashe. When Mandela later visited New York, he wanted to meet Ashe. President Mandela embraced him and told him how much of an inspiration his book was to him while he was in prison.

It took Ashe many years to write *A Hard Road to Glory*, but he was dedicated to telling a story that had received little attention. Herb Boyd said of Ashe's book, "[It's] just a remarkable collection of the kind of contributions that black athletes made in this country. He brought the missing pages of African American history to us." Ashe always believed in the value of education and wanted all people, but especially blacks, to be educated about the history of their own race. In researching his book, he became deeply concerned by the fact that only one in four black college athletes at the Division I level graduated from college. He started the Athletes Career Connection and the African-American Athletic Association to mentor young black athletes and emphasize the importance of attaining a college education. Ashe's passion for helping people never seemed to end. He partnered with a legendary tennis instructor to form the Ashe-Bollettieri Cities program, and he started the Arthur Ashe Institute for Urban Health to develop innovative approaches to the problems facing urban areas across the United States.

Ashe accomplished most of these feats while struggling with his own health. In 1979 he suffered a heart attack and subsequently underwent quadruple bypass surgery, which ultimately led to his retirement from professional tennis in 1980. In 1983 he had another heart attack and underwent double bypass surgery. In 1988 he underwent brain surgery. At that time, tests revealed the biggest blow yet to his health. Ashe was HIV-positive. He also suffered from a rare infection of the brain called toxoplasmosis, one of the two dozen or so diseases associated with HIV. In other words, Ashe had AIDS. He learned all of this within a span of twenty-four hours.

At that time, being diagnosed with AIDS was a certain death sentence. Because Ashe did not use intravenous drugs, was not gay, and had been faithful to his wife, doctors were able to trace the origins of the virus to a blood transfusion that he received after his 1983 bypass surgery. At that time, blood was not tested for HIV, and Ashe became part of the two percent of AIDS patients who contracted the disease through a blood transfusion. In 1985 the U.S. government began testing all blood banks for HIV—a few years too late for Ashe.

Because Ashe was a private person and did not want to alarm his young daughter, he planned to keep the news of his AIDS out of the public arena. However, in 1992 a national newspaper threatened to go public with this personal information. With a great deal of anxiety and trepidation, Ashe held a news conference to tell the world that he had AIDS. At the time of the press conference, he had less than one year to live. However, many would argue that Ashe is better known for what he did in the last ten months of his life than what he did in the previous forty-nine years. He took the same passion he had for other causes and focused it on AIDS and its many victims. At a time when the world had very little understanding, tolerance, and compassion for people with AIDS, Ashe forced Americans to face their prejudices and become more fully informed about the disease. Legendary news commentator Barbara Walters had this to say: "After Arthur Ashe spoke out, people said, 'It can happen to anyone.' And I think it changed people's understanding of AIDS and who could get it."

The former tennis star soon founded the Arthur Ashe Foundation for the Defeat of AIDS. Like a true champion, he was not just out to do battle with the disease, he wanted the foundation to conquer AIDS. He once said, "Maybe there's not a cure for AIDS in time for me, but certainly for everyone else, and that should be enough to maintain this hope." Aside from conquering AIDS, he wanted Americans to have a better understanding of the ways the disease was spread and to be more tolerant of those who had the disease. When AIDS first surfaced, sixty percent of those who suffered from it were gay males, and another twenty-three percent were drug users who had acquired it by sharing needles. Therefore, many Americans thought those who had AIDS deserved it because they had engaged in what were widely considered to be immoral acts. Some even thought this was God's way of exacting punishment on sinners. Ashe spent much of his time debunking the myths of AIDS, saying, "One of the things we really need to get away from is a moral judgment that somehow AIDS is God's retribution or revenge on the sins of society or a certain group of people."

It was also a time when people were afraid to shake hands with or breathe the same air as somebody with AIDS because of the unfounded fear that it was some kind of germ that could be passed from person to person. Ashe was one of the first people to dispel some of these misconceptions. He said, "You can kiss me, you can hug me, you can shake my hand, you can drink out of the same glass. I can sneeze on you, I can cough on you, you're not going to get it from me." Ashe even had a rare opportunity to speak to the United Nations about the disease.

Until his death, Ashe worked tirelessly to educate people about the realities of AIDS. Author Herb Boyd noted, "So long as he could be articulate and had the strength to get up to the lectern, I mean right down to his final days, he was still out there waging the struggle." Unfortunately, Ashe lost his personal struggle with AIDS, dying in 1993. His foundation, however, continues to raise millions of dollars to fight AIDS on behalf of the 38 million people with the disease worldwide. Ashe would be devastated to know that an estimated twenty million people worldwide have died of AIDS and an estimated five million more became infected with HIV in 2003. But he would be encouraged by the recent advances in the treatment of the disease.

Many honors have been bestowed on Arthur Ashe. After his death, the main stadium at Flushing Meadow, the site of the U.S. Open, was named after him. Each year on the day preceding the U.S. Open, children flock to this site to celebrate Arthur Ashe Kids' Day and commemorate the spirit and legacy of the late tennis player. Twelve years after Ashe's retirement from tennis, *Sports Illustrated* named him Sportsman of the Year. Using the photograph from that magazine cover, the U.S. Postal Service plans to release a commemorative postage stamp in 2005 to honor him.

In 1996 Ashe's hometown of Richmond honored him with a twelve-foot bronze statue on Monument Avenue, one of the city's best-known and most historical streets. Ashe's likeness stands among statues of the Civil War's confederate leaders in a city that at one time would not allow a black child to play tennis against a white child. "Arthur Ashe is a true Virginia hero, and he belongs here," said his brother, Johnnie Ashe. Even after his death, Ashe is still creating change and having a positive impact.

Ashe did so much for humankind and was a role model for us all. He had many talents—he was an excellent athlete, a scholar, a social activist, a teacher, a writer, a sports analyst, a husband, and a father. In the last year of his life he wrote his autobiography, *Days of Grace*. The following are some of the last words he ever wrote: "Whatever happens, I know that I am not going to be alone at the end. I have invested in friendship all my life. I have been patient and attentive, forgiving and considerate, even with some people who probably did not deserve it. I made the investment of time and energy, and now the dividends [are] being returned to me in kindness." He knew that the more you give, the more you receive. Never was this truer than for Arthur Ashe.

Some people believe that no modern athlete since Ashe has stepped up to make such enormous contributions to humankind. As sociologist Harry Edwards said, "There's a tremendous deficit in the dialogue around American sport as a consequence of Arthur not being here. Nobody has really replaced him. That bridge is out, it's gone." Even Ashe's widow, Jeanne Moutoussamy-Ashe, is afraid that his legacy might get lost in this era of big money and instant gratification. She reminds us, "Arthur used his life to move us all forward. The young people today don't really know Arthur. I think it would be just an absolute travesty if they only thought of him as a tennis player who died of AIDS." After reading this chapter, I hope you know much more than that about the great Arthur Ashe.

Pat Tillman

Duty

On December 7, 1941, "a date which will live in infamy," Japan launched a sneak attack on Pearl Harbor. The next day America declared war on Japan. Angry American citizens began signing up to serve their country in the armed services. Professional athletes were no exception. Among the eight million Americans who served were 500 major league baseball players and 638 professional football players. Because so many athletes had enlisted in the military, baseball commissioner Kenesaw Mountain Landis considered shutting down the game until the war ended. Professional football teams were so depleted that some owners combined players just to field a team. The Philadelphia Eagles and Pittsburgh Steelers merged to become the Phil-Pitt Steagles. Football practices were held in the evenings to allow athletes to contribute to the war effort by working in defense-related factories during the day. Baseball games were played mostly at night to allow blue-collar workers to attend, thereby boosting national morale. Americans knew the meaning of duty and sacrifice during wartime, and professional athletes did their part as well.

Baseball Hall of Famers Joe DiMaggio, Warren Spahn, Hank Greenberg, and Bob Feller proudly served in the military. Ted Williams, widely considered to be the best hitter of all time, enlisted twice. He served as a Navy pilot during World War II and again during the Korean War, sacrificing five prime years of his career for his country. Professional football players also felt a call to duty. Heisman Trophy winner Nile Kinnick died while serving in the military when his plane crashed just short of the aircraft carrier *Lexington*. Maurice Britt and Jack Lummus fought so valiantly that each received our country's highest honor, The Congressional Medal of Honor. Lummus almost single-handedly wiped out three Japanese bunkers and was subsequently killed when he stepped on a land mine on Iwo Jima. Britt was seriously wounded in a firefight in Italy, and according to Army reports, "Despite his wounds he personally killed five and wounded an unknown number of Germans, and wiped out one enemy machine gun." Britt would never play professional football again.

Nearly sixty years after the attack on Pearl Harbor, on September 11, 2001, al-Qaeda terrorists hijacked four airplanes and crashed them into the World Trade Center, the Pentagon, and into a field in rural Pennsylvania. A combined 2,992 people were killed in these attacks, compared to 2,388 people who were killed at Pearl Harbor. Americans were once again outraged by an attack on U.S. soil. President George W. Bush immediately called for a "War on Terror" and Congress passed a resolution authorizing the president to use military force. Americans expressed their patriotism by proudly displaying the flag and by donating money to the families of the victims. And, just like in 1941, many people began to enlist in the armed forces. There was, however, one notable difference this time around. Only two professional athletes signed up to fight for their country—Pat and Kevin Tillman.

When the brothers enlisted, Pat Tillman was a starting safety for the Arizona Cardinals. His little brother, Kevin, was a minor league pitcher in the Cleveland Indians organization. In recognition of their desire to serve a greater good outside the world of sports, both brothers were recipients of the Arthur Ashe Courage Award, presented during the 2003 ESPY Awards. True to their modest nature, they declined to attend the ceremony, sending their younger brother, Richard, to accept the award on their behalf. They did not want to call any attention to themselves for their decision to wear a different uniform. They wanted no special privileges, no preferential treatment. In the acceptance speech, Richard said, "Pat and Kevin don't think they are better than anybody else. They do not feel that the soldiers fighting alongside them are giving any less than they are."

While this is true, unlike the other soldiers, Pat Tillman left behind a $3.6 million pro football contract when he enlisted. Many people could not understand why he would sacrifice his dream of playing in the NFL for an annual salary of $17,316 in the armed forces. Tillman declined all interview requests once he joined the Army, so no one can definitively say why he joined or what he hoped to accomplish. However, based on his reaction to the attacks of 9/11 and the kind of person he was, we can make a few educated guesses. First, his decision to enlist was not a publicity stunt. If it had been, he would have accepted the offers of multi-million dollar book deals, movie contracts, and commercial endorsements. His face and image would have been everywhere. To the contrary, Tillman was a person with deep convictions who made decisions based on principle. The clearest answer as to why he joined the Army Rangers came from Joseph Bush, an Air Force sergeant who just happened to run into his football hero when both were serving in Saudi Arabia. Bush asked the same question many others had: "Why would you give up the NFL for a life like this?" Tillman's answer: "For the love of my brother. And for the love of my country." Jim Rome, an ESPN analyst, said, "When he gave up his career to join the Rangers, people said, 'How can he do that?' Pat said, 'How can I not?'"

Tillman might not have provided the public with a definitive answer as to why he enlisted, but judging from his emotional reaction on September 11, 2001, it is safe to assume this event played a significant role. On that terrible Tuesday morning, Tillman watched the events unfold from the Phoenix Cardinals media lounge. He watched the towers collapse and his fellow Americans perish in the rubble left behind. He was angry, emotional and helpless—unable to do anything to stop it. In the ensuing days, Tillman seemed profoundly influenced by the terrorist attacks. "I was dumbfounded by everything that was going on," he said. "In times like this, you stop and think how good we have it. I have always had a great deal of feeling for the flag, but you don't realize how great of a life we have over here.... A lot of my family has gone and fought in wars, and I haven't really done a damn thing as far as laying myself on the line like that." Eight months later, in May 2002, Tillman joined the Army. Eighteen months after that, Tillman completed a grueling training program at the Army Ranger School to become a member of the world's best light-infantry fighting force. In April 2004 Tillman found himself in Osama bin Laden's backyard fighting terrorists. Three weeks later, on April 22, 2004, Tillman was accidentally killed by someone in his own platoon during a firefight, leaving behind a grieving widow and thousands of fans.

A swarm of controversy has surrounded Tillman's last moments. His parents have been particularly upset with the way the military covered up the facts related to his death. When the initial reports of the firefight were released to the public, they made Tillman look like a battlefield hero. He was even posthumously awarded the Silver Star and the Meritorious Service Medal. Unfortunately, most of this was just a fabrication of the truth. The truth is that Tillman entered a dangerous section of Afghanistan with a small detail of Rangers to recover weapons and hunt down al-Qaeda terrorists. His platoon was ordered to split up into two squads. At some point in the mission, members of the other squad got confused and began shooting on Tillman's position. Tillman did everything he was supposed to do to identify himself as an American to his fellow Rangers, but he was unsuccessful. Unfortunately, friendly fire is a terrible reality of war—accidents happen. Regardless of how he died, it should not overshadow his convictions to fight for his country and make the world a safer place.

To date, more than 3,400 U.S. soldiers have died in the Middle East, but this was the first time many Americans could associate a face with one of the casualties. Tillman was known as the famous football player who gave up a pro career to fight for his country. His death seemed to put things in perspective, forcing Americans to face the realities of war. "In sports we have a tendency to overuse terms like courage and bravery and heroes, and then someone like Pat Tillman comes along and reminds us what those terms really mean," commented Michael Bidwell, vice president of the Arizona Cardinals. Those who knew him mourned his loss. "What we lost in terms of a person is really something that a lot of us would like to have, those kinds of convictions and the kind of character and attitude that he had about living daily life," said Larry Marmie, former defensive coordinator of the Cardinals.

Tillman lived life to the fullest. He was a man of substance who had that "it" quality—something intangible that you can't quite put your finger on, but you know it when you see it. Jake Plummer, a former teammate, tried to define this elusive quality in Tillman. "He was something special.... He had an intensity you can't describe. It was an inspiration for everybody who played with Pat." Marc Flemming, a former high school teammate, added, "He had a passion for what he did until the day he died. That is something most men never will achieve." Marmie said, "The real sad part is that they [Americans] didn't really know Pat Tillman as a person." The real Pat Tillman story isn't about how he died, but rather how he lived.

Pat was a bicentennial baby, born on November 6, 1976. His father, Pat Tillman Sr., was an attorney. His mother, Mary, was a substitute teacher. Pat was the oldest of three boys. The family lived in a suburb of San Jose, California. During his youth—and for that matter, as an adult too—Pat marched to the beat of his own drum. It was widely reported that his favorite word was "dude," and his attire usually consisted of a pair of cutoff shorts, a T-shirt, and a pair of flip-flops. If he was not riding his mountain bike or using his roller blades, he might have been climbing trees or jumping off the porch roof. Apparently, rambunctious behavior was par for the course for this youngster. According to his dad, "He has always liked testing himself."

Pat's competitive edge served him well when he began playing sports at Leland High School, a large school with a strong history of athletic achievement. Because he had not hit puberty by the time he entered high school, Pat was a scrawny-looking freshman. Nonetheless, he was a good athlete and excelled in baseball and football. However, when Pat was told by the baseball coach that he would not make the varsity baseball team, but was welcome to play on the junior varsity squad, he told the coach that he had decided to focus solely on football. The coach responded, "Pat, that's probably a bad decision, because if you're going to play a college sport, it will have to be baseball. It certainly won't be football!" The baseball coach turned out to be the first of many people Pat would prove wrong in the upcoming years.

At the end of the football season, Pat was one of four freshmen approached by the varsity coach and invited to move up to the varsity team for the next year. The other three students declined because they preferred starting on the junior varsity team, as opposed to potentially riding the bench on the varsity team. Pat, however, was quick to accept the offer. He loved a challenge and did not let uncertainty or fear rule his life. He continually set high expectations for himself and raised the bar at every opportunity.

In one playoff game, for example, Leland was ahead 55-0 at halftime. Before the second half kickoff, the coach told his star player, "Pat you're done for the day, and I don't want you playing any offense or to play any defense." A few seconds later, Pat ran onto the field to take his place as the kick-returner on special teams. He returned the kick-off for a touchdown. As he walked to the sidelines, Pat confidently looked his coach in the eye and said, "You mentioned nothing about special teams." To prevent any further misunderstandings, the coach confiscated his helmet and shoulder pads for the remainder of the game.

By the time Pat was a high school senior he was a legitimate football star. He averaged 10.9 yards a carry as a fullback and led the team in tackles with 110 as a linebacker. His team finished 12-1 and Pat was named the Central Coast Section co-player of the year. An opposing coach spoke highly of Pat's athleticism. "He is a man among boys. He reminds me of Ronnie Lott on defense. I really believe he's the best overall athlete I've seen in my coaching career."

Despite his dominance on the football field, only three Division 1-A schools expressed any interest in Pat. One of those schools was Arizona State University. Head coach Bruce Snyder later explained his initial reluctance to offer Pat a scholarship. "I kept looking at this guy that did not fit the physical profile. He was too short, too slow, didn't weigh enough. But whenever I watched tape, he was always the best player on the field." At 5'11" and 195 pounds, he was a classic "tweener"—too small to play linebacker and not fast enough to play cornerback. During a campus visit, however, the coaches were struck by Pat's personality and ambition. Without a doubt, his potential could not be measured with a scale, a yardstick, or a stopwatch. His heart and character clearly outweighed his physical stature. The Arizona State coaches became convinced that Pat had what it took to succeed at the collegiate level. They offered him the last scholarship of 1994.

Pat Tillman did not look or act like a typical college jock. He grew his hair well below his shoulders, earning the nicknames "Goldilocks," "Blondie," and "Braveheart." If he had not been so driven and focused, he could have easily been confused with a surfer-dude waiting for the next big wave. But he was driven and focused—and not just with football. His grade point average for his first three semesters at ASU was consistently at 3.5 and above. Tillman was not enrolled in the typical blow-off classes that many big-time college athletes take either. He was a marketing major and aced courses in accounting, economics, statistics, and communications.

Tillman was named the *Sporting News* Honda Scholar-Athlete of the Year and was named to several Academic All-American teams. At a time when the average student is on the five-year plan, Tillman graduated in three-and-a-half years with a GPA of 3.84. When asked how he managed to be so successful in academics, he said, "It's something that if you want to do it, you can do it. The classes are there to take. I just had the motivation to do it."

Tillman was on an accelerated course with football too. The coaches at ASU had wanted him to redshirt his first year, meaning he would sit out his first year without losing a year of eligibility. This practice allows freshmen to mature on the bench and have more playing time as fifth-year seniors. When presented with this option, Tillman was not interested. "Coach, you can play me or not play me," he said, "but I'm only going to be here four years. And then I've got things to do with my life." In another interview, he explained, "There's a lot of opportunity out there in this country, and I'm going to reach for the sky.... I want to be a billionaire eventually and do whatever I want. I'm not exactly sure how I'm going to do it, but I'll figure it out."

With dreams like that, Tillman wasn't worried about a simple thing like playing time. His only goal was to do his best. Thanks to his hard work, Tillman quickly became one of the best special-teams players and even started a game at linebacker as a freshman. As a sophomore, he continued to do everything that was asked of him and became the team's sixth-leading tackler.

Many people did not know what to think of this free-spirited guy. "When it was cool to have his hair long, he wore it short. When it was cool to have it short, he wore it long," said his brother-in-law, Alex Garwood. On the field, Tillman was known as the "hit man" but off the field he was a deep thinker. Even Tillman's road-game roommate believed he was misunderstood. "People thought he was a crazy guy, but I would try to tell people that Pat was one of the most level-headed guys I know," he said.

Still, Tillman was unusual in many ways. During training camp the team would head to the mountains and hold twice-a-day practices. During the breaks, most players were so exhausted that they found a quiet place to relax. Not Tillman. He spent his leisure time climbing fifty-foot cliffs and jumping into the water below. During the season, he would regularly climb a 200-foot tower—in his flip-flops no less—just to clear his mind and contemplate the future. No wonder people thought he was crazy. He also read everything he could get his hands on. He would then test his knowledge by choosing controversial sides of an issue and debate his friends just for the fun of it.

On the field, Tillman was becoming one of the best

linebackers in the country and making a significant impact on ASU team. The highlight of his college career was the team's upset of the defending national champion Nebraska Cornhuskers, ending their twenty-six-game winning streak. ASU finished the regular season undefeated at 11-0, but lost the Rose Bowl when the Ohio State Buckeyes scored a go-ahead touchdown with nineteen seconds remaining on the clock. It was a heartbreaking way to lose the national championship.

While the ASU football team did not fare as well during Tillman's senior year—finishing the season at 9-3—he led the team in tackles and was named Pac-10 Defensive Player of the Year. Not bad for an undersized linebacker who was only recruited by three schools. According to one teammate, Tillman had more important qualities than size. "You see a guy like that smashing people, it makes me want to do the same thing," his teammate said. "It's all about heart. He's just about the strongest person, mentally, I've ever met."

If people thought Tillman was too small and too slow for college football, imagine what the pros thought of him. He would have to prove them wrong too. In the 1998 NFL draft, 243 players were selected over the course of seven rounds. The Arizona Cardinals selected Pat Tillman as the 228th pick in that final round. "When we drafted Pat, we had three picks in the seventh round, the last round of the draft, and we picked him with the 7C pick," said Vince Tobin, former head coach of the Cardinals.

Tillman came that close to not realizing his dream of playing in the NFL. If it weren't for his tenacity and work ethic, he wouldn't have been drafted at all. Because the Arizona Cardinals and ASU shared the same football stadium, several of the coaches had agreed to observe Tillman run some drills. This fifteen-minute workout turned into a forty-five-minute ordeal because Tillman wouldn't let them leave until he performed every drill to the best of his ability. "He wouldn't quit," one coach said. "By the time the workout was over, his shirt had come off and he was diving onto the ground. That type of commitment, that type of drive, that type of inner passion that he had, showed through after we took him in the seventh round."

Tillman did not care what round he was drafted—he just wanted an opportunity to prove himself. And he did. The first thing the Cardinals did was move him to free-safety, a position he had never played. Without missing a beat, Tillman hit everything that moved and, against all odds, became the team's leading tackler during the pre-season. Apparently that's all the maturation he needed because the Cardinals named him as the starter for the first game of the season. Tillman ended up being the spark that set fire to the team. His head coach said, "I had an affinity for Pat because his toughness was contagious. Other players fed off of him, and that's not just a line."

The Cardinals made the playoffs that year for the first time in fifteen years and won their first playoff game in fifty-one years. In 2000, Tillman set a team record with 224 tackles. It was about this time that Tillman began to get attention from other NFL teams. The St. Louis Rams reportedly offered Tillman a contract worth $9 million. He turned down the opportunity to make more money, opting to stay with the Cardinals. His reasons were simple. "I felt loyalty to the coaches," he explained. "I've come a long way, and it's because of them." Tillman added later, "I try not to make decisions based on money." Loyalty was one of many character traits Tillman possessed.

While many people talk about leading a principled life, Tillman lived one. According to one of Tillman's former professors at ASU, Michael Mokwa, "If you look at Pat's life, his theme always was to look deep into himself and determine what was right or wrong, good or bad, appropriate or not appropriate, and then to generate his values through this." Mokwa added, "Once he grabbed a value, he just relentlessly stuck with it and turned it into action."

Material possessions did not mean much to Tillman. When other NFL players were buying flashy cars and living in mansions, he was still driving his old Volvo station wagon and living in a modest home. Not only that, he frequently rode his beat-up Schwinn bicycle to work in the stifling 115-degree Arizona heat. For most professional football players, the rigor of an NFL season is demanding enough. Not so for Tillman. He challenged himself by competing in triathlons and marathons in his spare time. He thrived on competition and loved to push himself to the limit. "Doing stuff like this gives me something to focus on," he said. "I feel like a bum not doing anything in the off-season."

Tillman was admirable but not perfect. Like anyone else, he made his share of mistakes. When he was seventeen, for example, he came to the rescue of a friend who was attacked by an older man outside a pizzeria. In defending his friend, Pat used more force than he should have and was later arrested for felonious assault. He pled guilty and spent thirty days in a juvenile detention center. While it was a noble gesture for him to defend his friend, Pat realized he had made a mistake in going too far. "I'm proud of that chapter in my life," he maintained. "I'm not proud of what happened, but I'm proud that I learned more from that one bad decision than all the good decisions I've ever made.... It made me realize that stuff you do has repercussions." He apologized, took responsibility for his mistake, and learned from it. He was given a second chance, and he made the most of it.

Unfortunately, there are no second chances when it comes to war. If Tillman had not been killed in Afghanistan, there is no limit to what he might have accomplished. His former college roommate thought Tillman's life was going to lead to something big. "If Pat were still alive and had made it out of that thing in Afghanistan, he would be back here trying to change stuff, trying to make things better by running for office or something like that," he said. "I believe he was going to run for some high office, if not president." Tillman possessed the power to change people, according to his brother-in-law, Alex Garwood. "Man, I spent just a few hours with that guy having a couple of beers, and he changed the way I think about life. He made me want to be a better person."

Radio broadcaster Jim Rome, master of ceremonies at Tillman's memorial service, put things into perspective. He said, "Pat is a hero.... I can't wait to sit my son down and tell him how much I admire Pat and tell him about the legendary Tillman intensity, his hunger, his desire.... I don't want to be like Mike [Jordan]. I want to be like Pat. I wish I would have spent more time with Pat because Pat's the man I want to be. Pat's the man we should all want to be."

Many other prominent people attended Tillman's memorial service and gave moving tributes. Maria Shriver, California's First Lady, said, "He was a glorious and shining example of honor, service, and devotion to a cause and a power much greater than himself." Senator John McCain, no stranger to war himself, had these words to say: "Pat's best service to his country was to remind us all what courage really looks like and that the purpose of all good courage is to love. He loved his country and the values that make us exceptional among nations." Dave McGinnis, former Cardinal head coach, talked about Tillman's character. "There was never a question where Pat Tillman stood. The character of a man is a very valuable thing.... The character of a man is his ability to make a decision and stand by it. Pat defined the word 'character.'" Finally, veteran football coach Lyle Setencich left Pat's friends and family with these words: "God bless Pat Tillman. God bless Pat Tillman."

There are many lessons we can learn from the life of Pat Tillman. He demonstrated the importance of having a dream and working hard to reach it, regardless of what others might say along the way. A strong belief in yourself can overcome the criticism of those who do not believe you can achieve your goal. Thanks to self-confidence and hard work, Tillman was an overachiever in every facet of his life.

He also demonstrated that true happiness comes from leading a principled life. He valued the ideals of loyalty, modesty, and duty over material possessions, fame, and self-gratification. Tillman applied these principles to every decision in life and earned respect from others in the process. He was not afraid to be his own person. Tillman was unconventional and free-spirited, and it served him well.

Finally, the story of Pat Tillman reminds us that words like sacrifice and hero have real meaning and should not be used lightly. America was saddened by the loss of this hero in wartime, but we should be grateful that he and other brave men and women are willing to sacrifice so much for their country. For his heroism and sense of duty to his county, we owe Pat Tillman a debt of gratitude.

Nancy Reagan

Loyalty

A century ago, divorce was virtually nonexistent, with less than five percent of marriages ending that way. Flash forward one hundred years and divorce is commonplace in American culture. Nearly fifty percent of all marriages that took place in the year 2000 will end up in divorce court. Yet during the last century, wedding vows have more or less stayed the same. Most couples still make the following vow while standing at the altar: "I take you to have and to hold from this day forward, for better, for worse, for richer, for poorer, in sickness and in health, to love and to cherish in good times and in bad until death do us part."

Despite the tears and emotion that typically accompany these words, Americans do not seem to value their wedding vows as much as they did a century ago. The vows do not say, "I take you until I'm relatively unhappy, until you make me mad, or until I find somebody better," although that seems to be the prevailing attitude toward marriage today. Every marriage, without exception, has high points and low points. To make it through the low points requires patience, sacrifice, and loyalty from both partners. Unfortunately, these character traits are at odds with a society that revolves around instant gratification. For the past several decades everything in America has become faster, easier, and more convenient. Relationships, however, still require old-fashioned hard work to make them successful. No new invention is going to change that fact.

Nancy and Ronald Reagan understood the meaning of their marital vows and knew what it took to make a marriage work.

They never wavered in their commitment and love for one another. While this chapter focuses on Nancy Reagan, the two were very much a team. Ronald Reagan took the lead in the couple's public life, but they were equals in their private life. Theirs is a love story of two people who respected and valued each other. Throughout their fifty-two years of marriage, their marital vows were tested but never broken. The Reagans' loyalty to each other should inspire all of us to value marriage and the seriousness of that sacred commitment.

If loyalty was key to the success of the Reagans' marriage, it is because Nancy learned the meaning of that trait when she was just a little girl. Nancy was born on July 6, 1921, to Edith Luckett, a single mom and stage actress. Edith joined a touring company to support herself and her daughter. As a baby, Nancy accompanied her mother as she traveled from play to play, city to city, in a laundry basket. Stagehands and cast members would take turns watching her while her mother was on stage. When Nancy was two and had outgrown the laundry basket, Edith made the difficult decision to leave Nancy with her Aunt Virginia and Uncle Audley in Bethesda, Maryland. The extended family took good care of Nancy, but she longed for her mother. For the next six years, Edith visited her daughter when she could. The highlight of those years for Nancy was the occasional trip to New York City, where she could see her mother perform on stage. Many children in similar situations might come to resent their parent or act out due to feelings of abandonment, but Nancy stayed loyal to her mother, believing that eventually they would be together. "I was thrilled when Mother came to visit and miserable when she left," Nancy said. "I understood that she had to work, and I knew that as soon as she could manage it, we would be together."

In 1929 Edith married a neurosurgeon from Chicago and ended her acting career. Her new husband's name was Dr. Loyal Davis. "He detested the name Loyal," Nancy recalled. "I always thought it suited him perfectly, for he was nothing if not loyal—to his family, his students, his profession, his patients, and above all, to his values." Nancy and her mother moved to Lake Shore

Drive to live with Loyal and his son, Richard, from a previous marriage. Nancy acquired the family she dreamed of and quickly became accustomed to her new lifestyle. Although at first she found it difficult to share her mother with the new man in her life, Nancy came to love her stepfather, and he officially adopted her when she was fourteen years old.

Nancy went on to attend Smith College in Massachusetts and became an actress. She dabbled in stage work, undoubtedly influenced by watching her mother as a child, but she preferred film. She signed with MGM Studios and made a dozen movies in all. However, Nancy has often claimed that her life did not really begin until she met Ronnie, as she affectionately referred to him.

Ronnie and Nancy began dating in 1950. He was an actor, as well as president of the Screen Actors Guild. In a time when women usually married young and divorce was rare, Ronnie and Nancy were somewhat unconventional. At the time of their marriage, Nancy was thirty-one years old and Ronnie was a forty-one-year-old divorced father of two. Circumstances and timing did not seem to matter, however, as they hit it off instantly. "Looking back now," Nancy reminisces, "I still can't define what it was about Ronald Reagan that made him seem so very perfect to me. I think we were just right for each other. I loved to listen to him talk. I loved his sense of humor. I saw it clearly that very first night: He was everything that I wanted." Ronnie felt just as strongly. "Nancy moved into my heart and replaced an emptiness that I'd been trying to ignore for a long time," he wrote in his autobiography. "Coming home to her is like coming out of the cold into a warm, fire-lit room. I miss her if she just steps out of the room."

The two were married on March 4, 1952, in a small, private ceremony. The first year of marriage was a difficult transition. Ronnie had difficulty finding work in the ever-changing film industry, and Nancy left MGM to raise their daughter, Patti, who was born later that year. The Reagans faced challenges not unlike those of most couples in their first year of marriage. Adjusting to living together, raising a family, and finding the money to survive can put a strain on any relationship. However, Ronnie eventually found work on television and was able to provide a comfortable income for the family. Their second child, Ron, was born in 1958.

A few years later Nancy and Ronnie decided to buy a ranch in California, mainly because of his love for the outdoors. Nancy too grew to love the land and the animals, and it became something they shared throughout their life. The Reagans' marriage was a partnership in which they saw each other as equals. Nancy once described it like this, "I don't ever remember once sitting down and mapping out a blueprint. It just became 'we' instead of 'I' very naturally and easily. And you live as you never have before, despite problems, separations, and conflicts. I suppose mainly you have to be willing to want to give."

Ronnie frequently sent Nancy love letters throughout their marriage. In 2001 Nancy published a collection of those treasured letters. They typically began with greetings such as "My Darling," "Dear First Lady," and "Dear Nancy Poo." Ronnie wrote to her in July of 1953, "Man can't live without a heart and you are my heart, by far the nicest thing about me and so very necessary. There would be no life without you nor would I want any." In March of 1963, Ronnie wrote, "There is really just an 'in between' day. It is a day on which I love you three hundred and sixty five days more than I did a year ago and three hundred and sixty five less than I will a year from now." Twenty-eight years into their marriage, Ronnie wrote, "I guess when I was young I thought marriage might be this way for a while: I never knew it could go on and on, getting better and better year after year.... I love you more than anything in the whole, wide world. I'm running for re-election as your own totally dedicated husband." Nancy had found a partner worthy of her loyalty, and the two made a great team, especially when Ronnie became interested in seeking political office.

Politics was a natural transition for Ronald Reagan. His interest in public service had been growing for several years, and in 1966 he was elected governor of California. Nancy supported her husband's new career even though it meant living a very public life and a reduction in their income. Ronnie had earned a six-figure salary for several years while working in television, but in 1967 the governor of California earned only $40,000 a year. "I supported Ronnie's decision to run for governor in 1966—not too much of a surprise," Nancy explained. "I always supported him in whatever he wanted to do. But as the campaign began, I felt a little uncertain about my own life in the political arena. It was a new and unfamiliar world for me."

The Reagans quickly adjusted to their new life in politics. Their favorite part was meeting new people each day and hearing their stories. "Ronnie and I now had new and different things to talk about every night at dinner," Nancy recalls. "And yet, for us as a couple, the heart of our life had not changed, and in fact, it never did; nor did our private time together.... We still shared everything together." Nancy fought hard to protect the private part of their lives. There were many people pulling her husband in different directions, and she tried to make sure that no one took advantage of him. "She's a builder and defender of her own," said Ronnie. "If you've seen a picture of a bear rearing up on its hind legs when its mate or one of its cubs is in danger, you have a pretty good idea of how Nancy responds to someone who she thinks is trying to hurt or betray one of hers."

In 1981 when Ronnie became the fortieth president of the United States, the media began to wonder if his wife played too big of a role in his professional life. It was often suggested that Nancy was influencing government or foreign affairs. Some speculated that Ronnie and Nancy actually shared the presidential power. Nancy has always insisted that this perception was false. She had her own duties as First Lady. And she believed that her close relationship with her husband was both beneficial and important. Despite criticism from the press and others, the Reagans' closeness, trust, and loyalty were a great comfort to both of them during his two terms as president. While other presidential marriages often became strained during the years spent in the White House, theirs flourished.

The Reagans, however, had their share of difficult times during the eight years that he served as president. The

President and Mrs. Reagan pose for a photo on the White House South Lawn in 1988. Photo courtesy of the Ronald Reagan Presidential Library [C49701-12].

assassination attempt in 1981 was by far the most traumatic. Nancy spent several days wondering if her husband's term in office would end the same way President Kennedy's had seventeen years earlier. Ronnie was shot on his seventieth day in office and he still had much to accomplish. After surviving surgery to remove the bullet, which was lodged one inch from his heart, Ronnie made a full recovery. For months after the shooting, Nancy protected her husband even more than usual, and she continued to worry throughout the remainder of his term. "I expected that the memory of the shooting would fade with time," she said, "but it never has. For the rest of Ronnie's presidency—almost eight more years—every time he left home, especially to go on a trip, it was as if my heart stopped until he got back."

The next eight years brought other challenges and more trying times. Both of Nancy's parents died, and she survived a bout with breast cancer. Ronnie survived colon and prostate cancer. "If Ronnie and I hadn't been so close, I don't know how we would have weathered the many sad and frightening experiences we had during the White House years," said Nancy. Little did they know as they left the White House for the final time in 1989, their biggest challenge lay ahead of them.

After twenty years in public life, the Reagans returned to California to begin their retirement. In Nancy's autobiography, published shortly after leaving the White House, she wrote, "And so as one door closes and another opens, we enter another phase of our lives. We're both busy giving speeches.... Ronnie is busy with his memoirs, and we're both getting reacquainted with California." They were able to enjoy their retirement for the first few years, but when Nancy wrote those words she had no idea what the next phase of their life together would bring or what was waiting for them behind that next door.

In 1995 Ronnie was diagnosed with Alzheimer's disease, a debilitating illness that steadily robs the memory. As the mind continues to fade, sudden mood changes, violent episodes, loss of recognition, and an inability to reason become daily hurdles. The worst part of the disease comes when the patient is unable to recognize loved ones or recall any significant memories, no matter how special they may be. It was only after Ronnie's diagnosis that the public came to truly understand the loyalty Nancy had to her husband and the bond that they shared. In previous years, her loyalty had been criticized as controlling or manipulative. In the 1980s, many feminists feared that Nancy was harming the women's movement by repeatedly putting her husband's interests above her own in their public life. However, millions of people came to admire Nancy as she continued to care for her husband as his illness progressed.

At that moment of Ronnie's greatest weakness, Nancy remembered the vows that she had taken more than forty years before—"for better, for worse, in sickness and in health"—and she never questioned what her role needed to be during her husband's remaining years. She would take care of Ronnie, just as she always had. Nancy once said of her husband, "Everything was always fine as long as he was there." Although Ronnie was physically with her for the next ten years, it was not long before his memory and personality were gone. The Ronnie she knew and loved could not be seen anymore in the shell of a person that remained. Alzheimer's is "really a very cruel disease, because for the caregiver, it's a long goodbye," said Nancy. Through it all, she pledged that she would, as always, remain by his side. "Theirs was an unalterable love," one biographer wrote.

Nancy created a haven for Ronnie at their home in California. She was with him every day and ate dinner with him in his room every evening, even after he no longer recognized her. For ten years she was his primary caregiver, rarely leaving the house for more than an hour or two at a time. She knew he found comfort in hearing her voice, even if that comfort came from a place buried deep within him.

In 2001 Ronnie fell and broke his hip. After he returned from the hospital, he never left the house again. Nancy brought in private nurses, which were not covered by government health insurance, to provide round-the-clock care for her husband. During Ronnie's final years, Nancy fiercely protected his privacy and dignity. She made sure that very few photos were taken or released during that time. She wanted the American people to remember Ronnie as a strong President, as the handsome former actor who led the country with conviction. She limited his visitors to only close friends and family. She knew that Ronnie would not want the world to see him in his diminished condition. Instead, to preserve his dignity, she bore most of the burden herself. "There are so many memories that I can no longer share," she said, "which makes it very difficult. When it comes right down to it, you're in it alone. Each day is difficult, and you get up, put one foot in front of the other and go—and love, just love," Nancy said. This was Nancy's life for ten years.

Ronald Reagan passed away on June 5, 2004, with Nancy by his side. Even though he had not opened his eyes for months or been able to recognize Nancy for years, Ronnie looked into Nancy's eyes for a few brief moments just before he died. It was as if he was saying "I love you and thank you" one last time. Then he was gone. Nancy described that last contact between them as "the greatest gift" he could have given her. Their daughter, Patti, described the moment like this: "It was his last act of love in this world and it was meant to cradle her until they are together again."

Finally it was time for the nation to say goodbye. A 200-page manual set the blueprint for the weeklong visitation and state funeral, the nation's first since 1973. Nancy wanted her husband's legacy to be honored appropriately, and Americans mourned along with her as they lined the procession route. Ronnie was buried at the Ronald Reagan Presidential Library in California, overlooking the Santa Susana Mountains. He had loved the view from the hill that was now his final resting place. Someday Nancy will join him there. According to Patti, "They will be laid to rest on a high hilltop, together as they were in life, a bit distanced from the rest of us because they were completed by each other."

Robert Watson, a presidential historian, said, "If there was no Martha Washington, there would have been no George Washington, and I think Nancy deserves a lot of credit in Ronnie's career—she was his promoter, supporter, cheerleader, pusher. And if it wasn't for her, we might be mourning the man who had a decent role as George Gipp in the movie *Knute Rockne* instead of the most influential American political leader of the last thirty years."

There will always be some speculation about just how influential Nancy was during Ronnie's years in politics, but there is no doubt that her deep sense of loyalty, trust, and commitment strengthened him in his quest to be a great leader. Nancy found that same strength in her husband's lifelong love when she stood by his bedside day after day and stayed true to the vows she had made decades earlier. "Shakespeare wrote plays about that kind of love," says Patti. "Poets, songwriters, novelists, have tried to describe it."

When Alzheimer's took its toll on Ronald Reagan, it robbed him of the memory of being President of the United States. He no longer recognized lifelong friends, and sadly, he was completely unaware of his and Nancy's fiftieth wedding anniversary on March 4, 2002. Whether he was able to comprehend it or not, however, it was Nancy's love and loyalty that sustained him over the last ten years of his life. Now that he is gone, it will be his love and their shared memories that will sustain Nancy.

Some parts of the Reagans' relationship may sound old-fashioned, and they were. But the principles of cooperation, respect, patience, and loyalty still set the foundation for any solid marriage, even in the twenty-first century. The Reagans understood that it took hard work to make a successful marriage last, and neither was willing to call it quits when times got tough. Nancy and Ronnie were very deliberate about making their marriage a priority. They protected their time together and did hundreds of little things, such as exchanging love letters, to keep the romance alive in their relationship. How many spouses do you know who have written enough love letters to fill up an entire book?

Psychologist Eric Fromm once said, "Love is an action and not a feeling," meaning that if we want satisfying relationships, we must put in the effort. If we fail to do that, the "feeling" of being in love fades and when it does, people often decide to divorce. It is easy to sustain a marriage during the good times, but the key is how you persevere through the difficult times.

If you fall in love and someday choose to marry, commit to your vows seriously, and remain loyal to your spouse through good times and bad.

Cal Ripken Jr.

Responsibility

In 1994 major league baseball players went on strike. For the first time in history, the World Series was cancelled. For many baseball fans, this action was unforgivable. They viewed the baseball players, many of whom make millions of dollars a year, as greedy and uncaring. Many fans vowed to stay away permanently from baseball. They refused to go to the ballpark or watch games on television. As a result, the average game attendance for baseball dropped twenty percent in the next year. However, even the most jaded fans could not turn their backs on the events that would unfold on September 6, 1995. Arguably the most prestigious record in baseball was about to be broken. Lou Gehrig, the original "iron man," played 2,130 games in a row for the New York Yankees from 1923–1939. To break Gehrig's record of consecutive games played, a player would have to play thirteen years without taking a day off. That would be like a student never missing a day of school from kindergarten through high school graduation. When people spoke of records that would never be broken, Gehrig's consecutive game streak was at the top of the list. Yet, Cal Ripken Jr. showed them that records are made to be broken.

The irony is that Ripken never set out to break any records. As he put it, "All I ever wanted to do was play well and play every day." In an era when overpaid athletes take themselves out of the lineup for a hangnail or a sore elbow, Ripken felt a responsibility to the game of baseball and to his teammates to play every day. He once commented, "When my team is out there on the field, I want to be with them." Most of his fans were hard-working people who could relate to his strong work ethic. Ripken did his job to the best of his ability and gave his full effort day in and day out. He was the consummate professional, never complaining after a loss nor calling attention to himself after a win. Cal Ripken Jr. was a loyal and dependable player who represented everything that is good about baseball.

As Ripken's playing streak began to approach Gehrig's record, the media coverage quickly became overwhelming. Every aspect of the streak was covered. When Ripken had answered every question posed by the media, reporters turned to relatives, friends, former teammates, and hotdog vendors to get their comments and opinions. Ripken estimates that he gave six interviews a day during the 1995 season. The interviews became so distracting to the team that a mock locker room was set up to accommodate the press. Ripken, a regular guy in many ways, had become as famous as any baseball player to ever play the game. And the fans couldn't seem to get enough of him. He would sign autographs for hours after the games ended. However, he never seemed to mind. "I do my best to get to as many as I can," Ripken said. "I'm happy and willing to give people as much time as possible." He thought of his time with fans as part of his responsibility as a major league ballplayer.

Breaking Gehrig's playing record was unlike breaking just about any other record in baseball. For instance, before Barry Bonds broke the single season home-run record, no one knew when, let alone if, he would indeed break the record. However, barring an unexpected injury, baseball fans knew that Ripken would break Gehrig's record on September 6, 1995, at Oriole Park at Camden Yards. President Bill Clinton was in attendance that day, along with 750 members of the press and a stadium packed with thousands of jubilant fans. In the bottom of the fourth inning, Ripken crushed a ball for a home run. Of that hit, Ripken said, "I nailed that pitch, and I knew right away it was gone. What a thrill that was!" When the final out of the fifth inning was made and the game was declared official, the fans went wild. For ten minutes, they were on their feet cheering and applauding their hometown hero. Ripken would periodically come out of the dugout to tip his hat to the crowd—the traditional way to say thank you and show respect in baseball. But this night was different. The fans wanted more. Finally a couple of teammates pushed Ripken onto the field, where he spontaneously took a lap around the bases. Along the way, he high-fived just about every fan in the front row. The celebration turned into a twenty-two-minute standing ovation filled with wide smiles and heartfelt tears. It was clear that baseball felt the same way about Cal Ripken Jr. as he felt about baseball.

In a speech after the game, Ripken thanked his family and paid homage to the late Lou Gehrig, who was struck down in his prime with ALS, a degenerative disease. Ripken concluded his speech with these words, "Whether your name is Gehrig or Ripken, DiMaggio or Robinson, or that of some youngster who picks up his bat or puts on his glove, you are challenged by the game of baseball to do your very best, day in and day out, and that's all I've ever tried to do."

To honor his marathon achievement, *Sports Illustrated* named Ripken the Athlete of the Year for 1995. He was also awarded the ESPY for Male Athlete of the Year in 1996. Everyone, it seemed, had something complimentary to say about Cal Ripken Jr., but Tom Hicks, owner of the Texas Rangers, might have expressed it best when he said, "He's one of the greatest ambassadors of the game we have ever seen. He's a great role model. He's a role model for baseball but also for the entire population."

Ripken played in 2,632 consecutive games in his career—a streak that covered sixteen years. On the last day of the 1998 season, Ripken elected to take himself out of the lineup. There was no big announcement or fanfare leading up to the game. Typical of Ripken, he just quietly asked the manager not to play him that night against the New York Yankees. When the Yankees realized the significance of the moment, they collectively stepped out of the dugout and tipped their hats to Ripken. It was their way of paying their respects. In return, Ripken tipped his hat toward them. Although he would play three more seasons, the streak was over. It was the end of an era.

Regardless of what Ripken does for the rest of his life, he will always be remembered for his playing streak. He is the iron man of baseball. To some extent, it's a shame that most people only know about that particular aspect of his life because the story behind the man is much more interesting. It is important to understand what made Ripken different from other talented baseball players. What drove him to be so dedicated to his craft? Why did he feel such a responsibility to the game and the fans when so many other pro athletes dodge this obligation? What events produced a man of such outstanding character and stamina?

Cal Ripken Jr. was born in 1960, while his father was a minor league player with the Baltimore Orioles. Unfortunately, Cal Ripken Sr. sustained an injury to his shoulder that permanently ended his dreams of making it to the big leagues. He quickly turned his attention to coaching, working his way through the minor leagues. As a result, the Ripken family moved to a different city nearly every season. Cal had an older sister and two younger brothers, and the four children lived in fourteen cities while growing up. Cal says that the biggest drawback of moving so often was the difficulty of making friends. The upside was that the family grew much closer because they had to rely on each other. The Ripken family was typical of that era, with Cal's mother staying at home to raise the children. Cal says that his mother ran a tight ship—he and his siblings were expected to meet certain standards, and mediocrity was not tolerated.

All the children loved to play sports. Cal played basketball, soccer, football, baseball, ping-pong—just about every sport you can think of. He developed a competitive edge and hated to lose. He still lists stubbornness as one of his dominant personality traits.

The Ripken family was not wealthy. The salary of a minor league coach is modest, and during the off-season, Cal Sr. had to take on extra jobs to make ends meet. At various times he worked at a lumberyard, a hardware store, and a pharmacy.

Those hard times taught Cal to do whatever was necessary to get ahead. His mom and dad provided a good example for their children under less than ideal circumstances. No one in the family complained or whined when things didn't go according to plan. All six of them kept plugging along and put forth their very best to contribute to the family.

When Cal was fifteen, his father landed a job in the major league as a scout for the Orioles. It was around this time that Cal was just beginning to take a serious interest in baseball. His dad's job gave Cal the opportunity to meet some of his heroes. On a few occasions he was allowed to shag some balls with the players during practice. The biggest asset to his dad's position, however, was having his father around to help him with the fundamentals of the game. For example, after a dismal freshman year in high school, Cal's dad took him into the batting cage to work on his swing. Cal's skills improved dramatically during his sophomore and junior seasons. By the time he was a senior he was hitting .496. Based on his success as a ballplayer, he decided to forgo college and entered the draft. As fate would have it, the Orioles used their second-round pick to select Cal Ripken Jr.

Due to the recent phenomenon of high school basketball players going directly to the pros and signing multi-million dollar contracts, many people might think Ripken became an instant millionaire as a big leaguer. Nothing could be further from the truth. In baseball, players usually spend several years trying to prove themselves in the minor leagues. For the record, Ripken made $100 a week during his debut season with a farm club in Bluefield, West Virginia. His life as a minor league ballplayer was anything but glamorous. Ripken lived in a boarding house with several of his teammates for $25 a week.

On opening day, Ripken made three errors and had a dismal performance at the plate. But, true to his upbringing, he did not give up. He was determined to get better. His body was still underdeveloped, so he made up for it by using his brain. He studied the opposing pitchers and kept notes on their strengths and weaknesses. Today that is standard procedure in baseball, but back then it was ingenious. Ripken's hard work and

Cal Ripken Jr. diving for a ball in his final season as a Baltimore Oriole.
Photo courtesy of Bill Wood and Ripken Baseball.

preparation paid off. He worked his way up through the system, from the Instructional League in St. Petersburg, Florida, to AA baseball in Charlotte, North Carolina, to the AAA club in Rochester, New York. In three years of professional baseball, Ripken played six hundred games, rarely missing a game, which is just the way he wanted it.

Finally, on August 8, 1981, Ripken was called up to the Baltimore Orioles. His excitement was dulled when he discovered that the Orioles already had a full infield, relegating him to a seat in the dugout chewing sunflower seeds. It was not exactly the start he was hoping for. However, in the off-season, a star player was traded, making room for Ripken at third base. When the 1982 season began, Ripken went into a severe batting slump. He couldn't even get a hit off of his own dad during batting practice. Nothing seemed to work. Finally, while playing against the California Angels, the great Reggie Jackson made it to third base and said to Ripken, "Look, don't let everyone else tell you how to hit. You could hit before you got here. Just be yourself and hit the way you want to hit." Those words of wisdom made all the difference in the world. Ripken began hitting again and won the Rookie of the Year Award for 1982. Earlier that year, in what seemed like an insignificant event at the time, Earl Weaver, the manager, decided to sit Ripken down for the second game of a doubleheader. Nobody knew it at the time, but that was the last time Cal Ripken Jr. would miss a game for the next sixteen years.

Over the course of his career, Ripken had many highs and lows. Some of his accolades include a World Series victory; being named a two-time MVP of the American League and two-time MVP in an All-Star game; and having nineteen consecutive All-Star appearances. He was also only the seventh player in history to hit 3,000 hits and 400 home runs, and he was voted the starting shortstop for the All-Century team. Ripken also endured many lows over the course of his career. He was a part of ten teams with losing records, including the 1988 team that lost 107 games. He had more strikeouts than any other Oriole in club history, and he endured many slumps at the plate. Through his humility and quiet determination, however, Ripken showed his fans that he could handle the good times and the bad.

When other professional athletes were denouncing the responsibility of acting as role models for their fans, Ripken openly embraced this status. Later he reflected, "Whether I liked it or not, my actions, I came to realize, influenced kids. Just as I had looked up to athletes when I was a boy, some kids were now looking up to me." He learned this the hard way early in his career. During the first inning of a game, he was ejected for arguing with the umpire. After the game Ripken learned that a young fan and his father had traveled all the way from Virginia just to watch Ripken play and that the boy cried the remaining eight innings. The story had a lasting impact on Ripken, and he learned to keep his anger under control and to maintain his composure regardless of the circumstances.

In 1987 Cal Ripken Sr. was promoted to manager of the Orioles. At the same time, Cal's brother Billy had been called up to the major league after working his way through the minors. The Ripkens became the first brothers in baseball to be managed by their father. When the boys were in high school, Cal Sr. was rarely able to watch them play because he was busy coaching. Now, as professionals, Cal and Billy could do what they loved in front of the man they loved. Cal always credited his father with teaching him how to play the game. The first public words he uttered after breaking Gehrig's record were, "Let me start by thanking my dad.... From the very beginning, my dad let me know how important it was to be there for your team and to be counted on by your teammates." As a child, Cal idolized his dad and wanted to emulate his can-do attitude. When asked about this father-son relationship, Cal Sr. commented, "I always talked to him about doing something the right way. He's the guy who had his priorities in the right order."

Throughout his life, Cal Ripken Jr. has put his family at the top of the list. In his autobiography, appropriately titled *The Only Way I Know*, Ripken says he enjoyed many incredible moments in his life, but cites four as the most special—three of which are related to his family. The first special moment was the day he married his wife, Kelly, whom he had met in an unusual way. While sitting in a restaurant one evening eating dinner with a teammate, Cal was approached by an attractive older woman who asked for his autograph. This scenario was not unusual, until the woman told Cal that he must meet her daughter, Kelly. Next to his autograph Cal wrote a clever note, which read, "To Kelly, if you look anything like your mother, I'm sorry I missed you."

A few weeks later, a young woman tapped him on the shoulder and thanked him for being so nice to her mother. Ripken quickly realized who she was and said, "You must be Kelly." Cal and Kelly dated for about a year before he decided to ask her to marry him. After cooking a romantic dinner for her one evening at his home, Cal invited Kelly out onto the balcony. While looking out at his backyard, he flipped a switch that illuminated several strands of Christmas lights that had been shaped into the question, "Will you marry me?" Cal dropped down to one knee and presented Kelly with an engagement ring. Apparently, the "iron man" of baseball has a soft heart. They were married on November 13, 1987.

Several years later, Ripken continues to make his marriage a priority. Each week during the off-season, he and Kelly have a date night. They spend a quiet evening together, regardless of what else is going on in their busy lives. They say that it helps to keep the romance alive in their relationship. Typically, they share dinner and a movie, which can be challenging given Ripken's celebrity status. He says that he usually waits in the car at the movie theater until Kelly gives him the signal that she has the tickets and the popcorn in hand. He then hurries into the theater as inconspicuously as he can. The effort is worth it, Ripken says. He recognizes that it is important to be "just a husband" sometimes.

Two of the other very special moments in Ripken's life came when his children were born. Like most fathers, Ripken says their births had a profound impact on him. He took to heart the responsibility of being a father to Rachel and Ryan, knowing that they were now depending on him and looking to him for support and guidance. He made them a priority in his life. For example, although Ripken feels a genuine responsibility to sign as many autographs as possible, when he is with his family, he politely declines, saying, "I'm just Rachel and Ryan's dad right now. I hope you understand."

Despite fortune and fame, Ripken never lost sight of his priorities. On the day that he broke Lou Gehrig's record, he started his day by driving his daughter to her first day of first grade. Ripken also requested that Ryan and Rachel be permitted to throw the ceremonial first pitch before the game that evening. After the game, he presented his children with his game jersey and showed them that he wore a special T-shirt underneath that read, "2130+ Hugs and Kisses for Daddy." In the middle of all the hype surrounding his record-breaking performance, Ripken didn't forget to tell his children how much he loved them.

Ripken is one of the few players in recent memory to play his entire career with one team. Like other talented players, he had several opportunities to make more money by playing for a different team. But when it came down to it, Ripken valued loyalty over money. He never got caught up in the ego-driven arguments about what he was worth as a ball player. He just played hard and let his numbers speak for themselves. His humility was refreshing to witness in a celebrity with his status, and it earned him respect from thousands of fans.

Even when he went into slumps, Ripken never agreed with the critics who told him he needed to rest. "That's always seemed like nonsense to me," he said. "Sitting out one or two innings isn't going to restore my energy. In fact, I perk up when I trot onto the field." Instead of resting, he simply worked harder. In 1990 when his batting average dropped to .250, several people said he was all washed up at the age of thirty. Ripken refused to accept that assessment. He built a gym at his house that included a batting cage, exercise equipment, and weight machines. He put forth what he called "total commitment" and began a regimented workout program. The next season he raised his batting average to .323 and was named the Most Valuable Player for the American League. He continued to apply the same work ethic to the game until the ripe old age of forty-one. Not many players continue to play professional baseball with gray hair. But there aren't many players as dedicated as Cal Ripken Jr.

In addition to family, Ripken has always felt a deep responsibility to his community. He and Kelly have hosted several fundraisers in the Baltimore area to help disabled children. They also started the Kelly and Cal Ripken Jr. Foundation to support literacy and health-related programs for young people. And because they passionately believe that every person should be able to read and write, they started an adult literacy project called the Ripken Learning Center. Finally, after breaking Gehrig's record in 1995, Ripkin set up the Cal Ripken Jr./Lou Gehrig ALS Research Fund. While many professional athletes are accused of taking more from the game than they give back, this is not true of Ripken.

People remember Ripken, the baseball player, for his dedication, loyalty, determination and humility. However, we should remember him for something more. Ripken displayed a sense of responsibility that is rare in the world today. He felt a responsibility to the game of baseball and to his teammates to give his best effort each and every day; he felt a responsibility to his fans and to society to give something back; and he felt a responsibility to his family to be a loyal and loving husband, father, son, and brother. To some people, he is seen as "old school" or a throwback to the way things used to be. Joe Torre, manager of the New York Yankees, alluded to this when he said, "Cal Ripken Jr. is a bridge, maybe the last bridge, back to the way the game was played." But Ripken shouldn't just remind us of how it used to be. He should be a living example of what is possible today. All it takes is a serious effort to put forth our very best—day in and day out. If we approach life with the same work ethic and sense of responsibility as Cal Ripken Jr., it would be amazing to see the difference each of us could make.

Ripken has been asked many times how he wants to be remembered. He says, "My answer is simple: To be remembered at all is pretty special. I might also add, that if I am remembered, I hope it's because by living my dream I was able to make a difference." No doubt about it, Mr. Ripken, you definitely made a difference. As a sign of respect, we tip our hat to you.

Oprah Winfrey

Compassion

The Oprah Winfrey Show is broadcast in 110 countries around the world. An estimated thirty million Americans tune in each day. These people invite Oprah Winfrey into their living rooms every afternoon to enlighten their minds and inspire their hearts. Despite competition from dozens of other talks shows over the years, *The Oprah Winfrey Show* has held the number-one spot in daytime television for eighteen years. The host, Winfrey herself, is witty, sincere, and personable. Actress Julia Roberts describes Oprah as "a girlfriend to the world." Her popularity transcends all ethnic, gender, age, and socio-economic barriers. During each show audiences can expect to laugh or cry as they learn more about issues and topics that affect their daily lives.

Oprah Winfrey is truly gifted in her ability to connect with other people. John Grace, a marketing expert, put it like this: "Her audience has come to believe Oprah is real and she is telling the truth." Winfrey has worked hard to earn this admiration. Her willingness to talk about the struggles she has faced throughout her life allow her to connect with ordinary people on an emotional level. Winfrey describes herself by saying, "I am a woman in progress. I'm just trying like everyone else. When viewers hear Winfrey talk about overcoming her own problems and conquering her inner demons, they are inspired to believe they can do the same thing.

Winfrey is more than just a talk show host. She is an actress, producer, author, and accomplished businesswoman. She has

---

assets currently valued at more than $1 billion, making her the sixth-wealthiest woman in the United States and the first African-American woman to reach that distinction. Oprah is by far the richest person selected for this book, but she also had the poorest upbringing. While the story of her success is remarkable, it is even more remarkable how she has used that success to make the world a better place. Winfrey's compassionate nature leads her to be generous with her time and money. According to *Business Week*, Winfrey has donated more than $175 million to worthy causes. She says, "My mission is to use this position, power, and money to create opportunities for other people." She remembers how opportunities were not so plentiful when she was growing up.

Oprah was born on January 29, 1954, in Kosciusko, Mississippi. Her mother intended to name her after Orpah, a woman mentioned in the Bible, but the name was misspelled on her birth certificate. Oprah's mother, Vernita, and father, Vernon, barely knew each other. Oprah characterizes their relationship as a "one-day fling under an oak tree." In fact, Vernita did not tell Vernon about her pregnancy until after Oprah was born. His notification came in the form of a birth announcement that was accompanied by a request for baby clothes.

Vernita had little money, so she moved in with her parents to raise Oprah. The young girl's formative years were spent on a tiny farm that had no electricity or indoor plumbing. To say that she was "dirt poor" is not an exaggeration, since the floors in her grandparents' house were made of just that—dirt. When Oprah was still a toddler, her mother left Mississippi to pursue a better-paying job in Milwaukee, Wisconsin. For the first six years of her life, Oprah was raised under the strict tutelage of her maternal grandparents. She quickly blossomed into an excellent student and an impressive public speaker. When she was just three, she recited a passage from the Bible in front of the entire congregation of her church. She loved to read and used books to dream about life outside of segregated Mississippi. Oprah was an overachiever in the classroom, completing homework assignments early and doing extra credit to earn high grades. She credits her grandmother for setting the foundation of her life. "I am what I am because of my grandmother," she says. "My strength. My sense of reasoning. Everything. All that was set by the time I was six."

Soon after her sixth birthday, Oprah joined her mother in Milwaukee. She lost the supportive home life she had known with her grandparents. Vernita worked long hours cleaning houses, which left Oprah unsupervised much of the time. At the age of nine, Oprah was sexually abused by an older cousin. Just a few years later, she was molested by a family friend and an uncle. Like many young victims of sexual assault, she did not tell anyone about the abuse until she was an adult. These traumatic events sent Oprah's life spiraling out of control. She became rebellious, running away from home, stealing money, and having sex with older boys. At the age of thirteen, Oprah became pregnant but did not tell anyone.

Vernita realized that she could not provide a proper home life for Oprah and asked Vernon to take her in. Oprah's father accepted the responsibility of caring for his teenage daughter, and she moved to Nashville, Tennessee, to live with him and his new wife. To conceal her pregnancy from her father, Oprah wore bulky sweaters and kept her distance. When she was seven months pregnant, Oprah was sent to a pediatrician because her "ankles were swollen." The pediatrician confirmed the pregnancy and told Oprah that she must to tell her father the truth. Years later, Oprah recounted the details to Barbara Walters. "The stress of having to tell my father sent me into labor," she said. "I delivered that child that day, and the child never left the hospital. It died." In a heart-to-heart talk with his daughter after the birth, Vernon told Oprah, "This is your second chance. You should make good on it."

Vernon Winfrey became the moral compass in his daughter's life, providing consistent structure and discipline. In addition to her schoolwork, she was required to read more and learn twenty new vocabulary words per week. "When my father took me in, it changed the course of my life," Winfrey later said. "He saved me." Her father might have provided the direction, but Oprah realized on her own that a positive attitude and effort could take her a long way in life. She once again began earning excellent grades. When she was sixteen, a local radio station agreed to pay her $100 a week to read the news on the air. The following year, she graduated from high school and was awarded a four-year academic scholarship to Tennessee State University. That same year, she was crowned Miss Black Tennessee.

Winfrey had talent as a broadcast journalist and it was just a matter of time before someone noticed. However, even she couldn't have imagined that her big break would come so soon. While still in college, Winfrey was offered the opportunity to anchor the news at a Nashville television station. She eagerly accepted, and at the young age of nineteen, she became the first African-American female news anchor in Nashville.

A few years later, in 1976, a much larger TV station in Baltimore recruited Winfrey to anchor their evening newscast. Her star was on the rise. There were just a few problems, though. The station manager in Baltimore told her that her hair was too thick, her eyes were too far apart, and her nose was too wide. In an attempt to "fix" some of these problems, she was sent to a prestigious New York salon for a makeover and a perm. The results were disastrous. The chemicals used on her hair made it fall out. Looking back on that experience, she said, "You come to learn a lot about yourself when you're bald and black and an anchorwoman in Baltimore."

To make matters worse, Winfrey was demoted for getting too emotionally involved in her stories. She had a habit of crying when she covered heartbreaking stories. She was reassigned to co-host a morning show called *People Are Talking*. As a serious newswoman, she was initially insulted by the offer to cover topics that she considered fluff. However, after the first show ended, she found herself thinking, "Thank God, I've found what I was meant to do. It's like breathing to me." The talk show format allowed Winfrey to be herself. While her laughter and tears once alienated the station's news producers, the same expressions of emotion were now endearing her to the public. For the next seven years, people in the Baltimore area were talking about Oprah Winfrey.

In 1984 Winfrey was offered an opportunity to relocate to the windy city to host *A.M. Chicago*. The job represented a huge opportunity because Chicago was one of the largest broadcast markets in the country. However, this time she wanted to be sure the station did not intend to "fix" her. Before accepting the position, Winfrey had a serious conversation with Dennis Swanson, general manager of the ABC affiliate in Chicago. She told him, "You know I'm black and that's not going to change, right?" Swanson responded with a grin, "I'm looking at you." But she wanted more assurance. "I have a weight problem I've been fighting all my life," she said. Swanson responded, "And so have I." Winfrey's new boss provided the affirmation she had been looking for since her career began. "You have a gift, young lady," Swanson said. "So just go on the air and be yourself."

Within a month, Winfrey's ratings were higher than those of Phil Donahue, the man who had been on top of the talk show industry for years. The following year the show was renamed *The Oprah Winfrey Show* and syndicated across the United States. In a savvy business move, Winfrey took a risk and decided to buy the rights to her show. She started a company called Harpo Productions—Harpo is Oprah spelled backward—and built a $20 million production facility to house the show. Instead of receiving a regular paycheck, she would now be responsible for writing the checks, deciding the content of the show, and producing it. In other words, she was now responsible for her own destiny. If the show failed, she could lose everything, but if it succeeded, she could potentially become a billionaire. Based on the fact that Winfrey is now included in *Forbes'* list of the 400 wealthiest Americans, it easy to guess how successful the show has become.

The Oprah Winfrey Show has earned more than $300 million for Harpo Productions, but the company is involved in many other ventures as well. In the 1990s, Harpo started small by initially producing made-for-television movies. A decade later, the company began publishing *O Magazine*, named for Oprah. The magazine has enjoyed the most successful beginning ever in the magazine publishing industry. It has approximately 2.5

million subscribers and brings in over $150 million each year. Every edition of the monthly publication features a glossy photo of Winfrey on the cover and is filled with inspirational and insightful articles that motivate people to improve their lives. Harpo Productions also owns a twenty-five percent stake in the Oxygen Network, a cable television channel that caters to women.

Winfrey acknowledges that it takes determination and hard work to stay on top. She freely admits that she is a workaholic. "This is all I do. I do this and I do it till I drop." Her day usually begins before dawn and doesn't end until long after the sun sets. She owns a lavish apartment on the fifty-seventh floor of a high-rise building that overlooks Chicago's Miracle Mile and Lake Michigan. However, for years she admits that she did not take the time to enjoy the view. "I'd come in to work at 5:30 in the morning when it was dark, and leave at 7:00 or 8:00 when it was dark," she said. "I went from garage to garage."

Winfrey is known for her attention to detail and high standards. The words "good enough" will likely never come out of her mouth as long as she is CEO of her company. She is personally involved in every facet of her TV show. She reads and re-reads every word in the magazine and does not give final approval until everything is perfect. Her longtime best friend and editor-at-large of *O Magazine*, Gayle King, says, "She's into every little niggly thing—the commas, the exclamation points." As a testament to her work ethic and attention to detail, Winfrey still allocates one entire afternoon each week to personally sign every check for the company.

While Winfrey prides herself on knowing how every penny of her company's money is spent, she is generous with her own resources. She articulates her philosophy on giving by saying, "Everything you do in your life comes back to you. I call it divine reciprocity." She remembers one particular event in her life that inspired this way of thinking. When she was twelve, her mother told her that she could not afford to buy her a Christmas present. However, on Christmas Eve three nuns came to the family's home to provide them with a turkey and a few toys to put under the tree. This compassionate act carried out by complete strangers now motivates Winfrey to put joy in the hearts of others.

Before Winfrey bought the rights to her TV show, several staff members requested raises from the previous management, only to be turned down. When she became CEO, she made sure every person on her staff received a Christmas bonus of $10,000. Once when she was on a movie set, she noted that while she and the other actors were treated to a lavish buffet every morning, the production staff brought fast food with them to the set. When Winfrey inquired about this discrepancy, she was told that the budget was too small to provide food for everyone. She promptly decided to use her own funds to provide food for the entire crew. These days, when Winfrey is invited to the White House to meet with presidents and other prominent members of society, she makes sure to venture into the kitchen to thank the staff that prepared the meal. Not many celebrities accompany her when she makes that detour to the kitchen.

Winfrey continues to donate more than ten percent of her income to charity. In addition to many anonymous donations, she has established several foundations. The Oprah Winfrey Foundation, established in 1987, supports the education and empowerment of women, children and families. In 1997, Winfrey started Oprah's Angel Network to inspire other people to donate to charity. To date, over $20 million has been collected and donated to worthy causes around the world. Finally, inspired by the nuns who selflessly gave her Christmas presents so many years ago, Winfrey has expanded her philanthropy through the Christmas Kindness South Africa initiative in 2002. She personally visited orphanages and rural schools in South Africa, providing gifts for 50,000 impoverished children. She also donated money to build schools and libraries in this impoverished region of the world. In 2007, she will kick off the Oprah Winfrey Leadership Initiative for Girls in South Africa. Winfrey is deeply committed to her foundations and the work they do around the world.

Closer to home, Winfrey participated in the Big Sisters program to mentor disadvantaged girls in the Chicago area. She invited the girls to her home for sleepovers, took them on field trips, and generously financed shopping sprees. The most important part of the job, however, was to be a role model. She tried to keep the girls on the straight and narrow. "When we talk about goals and they say they want Cadillacs, I say, 'If you cannot talk correctly, if you cannot read or do math, if you become pregnant, if you drop out of school, you will never have a Cadillac, I guarantee it!'"

Winfrey also mentored a thirteen-year-old boy, Kalvin, from the housing projects of Chicago. Despite the overwhelming obstacles in his life, Winfrey was hopeful that Kalvin could accomplish great things. She personally tutored the boy, helped his mother obtain her GED, and moved the family into a safer home. Inspired by their turnaround, she started a program called Families for a Better Life and personally donated $6 million to get the organization off the ground.

The Oprah Winfrey Show has always had a different feel than most daytime talk shows. When the show debuted in the 1980s, Winfrey admits she was guilty of covering "trashy" issues like the other talk shows, but even then, she says she was not trying to surprise her guests or shock the audience. "From the beginning, my philosophy has been that people deserve to come and to leave my show with their dignity," she explains. By the 1990s, Winfrey was tired of that type of show and disgusted with the talk show industry. In an interview, she tried to distance herself from the "trash pack" by explaining her philosophy on the subject. "A good talk show will stimulate thought, present new ideas, and maybe give you a sense of hope where there wasn't any—a feeling of encouragement, enlightenment. Inspire you," she said. Many fans believe it is this philosophy that has kept *The Oprah Winfrey Show* in the number-one slot for so many years.

The show continues to attract Hollywood's biggest stars, and Winfrey routinely lands big interviews, but her show is just as likely to feature the uplifting story of an ordinary person. She has produced shows, for example, on real-life heroes. On one

Oprah Winfrey meets President George H. W. Bush.
Photo courtesy of the George Bush Presidential Library [P04440-06A].

inspiring segment she interviewed three men who stopped their car to drag an unconscious stranger from his truck just before it exploded into flames. As the camera panned the audience during the segment, a dry eye was hard to find.

The theme for the show's 2004–2005 season was "Wildest Dreams Come True." Winfrey kicked off the season by giving away 276 cars to audience members. Everyone in the audience had been selected because they owned old, dilapidated cars and desperately needed new transportation. Winfrey arranged for Pontiac to donate the new cars and cover the cost of taxes for each one. When asked why she decided to give every member of her audience a new car, she replied, "Just because we can."

Winfrey also has great compassion and respect for educators, believing that they often do not get the gratitude they deserve. She recently invited an audience of teachers to her annual "Favorite Things" show. She then showered them with dozens of gifts. Each of the underpaid and overworked schoolteachers walked away with new merchandise worth thousands of dollars.

Winfrey has been recognized by her peers for the profound impact she has had on television and humanity. Edward Fritts, CEO of the National Association of Broadcasters, said, "Oprah has revolutionized daytime television and has brought a higher level of compassion and activism to the genre." Her awards are too numerous to count, but a few stand out. In 1998 the National Academy of Television Arts & Sciences presented Winfrey with a Lifetime Achievement Award. That same year *Time* named her one of the 100 most influential people of the 20th century. She also received the inaugural Bob Hope Humanitarian Award at the Emmy Awards in 2002. Finally, she received the 2004 Distinguished Service Award from the National Association of Broadcasters. Winfrey is appreciative of the awards and remains humble. "Believe me, my feet are still on the ground," she said. "I'm just wearing better shoes."

While Winfrey is a compassionate woman, she also emphasizes the importance of personal responsibility in people's lives. "My message is 'You are responsible for your own life'," she said. "Don't complain about what you don't have. Use what you've got. To do less than your best is a sin." She is happy to lend a helping hand to those who need it, but expects those she helps to take positive steps to better their own lives as well.

Over the course of her own life, Winfrey has worked through many difficult issues, including sexual abuse, racial and gender discrimination, and low self-esteem. She also struggled for many years to control her weight. However, she never felt sorry for herself but instead has worked diligently to overcome these obstacles.

Winfrey is an inspiration and a role model for others because she works hard to improve her own life. She applied her legendary work ethic to overcome her weight problems and maintain a healthy lifestyle. For example, she rises at 5:30 each morning to run forty-five minutes on the treadmill before she begins her long workday. Three days a week she adds thirty minutes of weight training to improve her strength and flexibility. In 1994 she pushed herself to train for and run a marathon. She has also changed her diet to include healthier foods and smaller portions. Finally, she has worked hard to understand the psychological issues related to her overeating. "For me, food was comfort, pleasure, love, a friend, everything. I consciously work every day at not letting food be a substitute for my emotions," she said in a moment of reflection. When someone with her wealth and status works this hard every day to improve herself, it inspires the average citizen to do the same.

It might surprise you to learn how a woman with nearly unlimited wealth, power, and influence spends her time. Winfrey's idea of fun is to curl up with a good book. She says, "Reading books is the single greatest pleasure I have." It seems that her father's directive to read more books when she was an adolescent had a profound influence on her life. She shares her love of reading with the world through her TV show and an online book club. She said, "The best thing about it is the thousands of letters from people who haven't picked up a book in twenty years." Several times a year she devotes a show to her favorite books and introduces new authors. As a testament to her influence on the buying public, books that are included in Oprah's Book Club are virtually guaranteed to sell an extra 500,000 to 700,000 copies.

Because of her overwhelming popularity, Winfrey has been forced to become more protective of her privacy over the years. She describes the price of fame this way: "You never, ever, ever have moments to yourself, and you're always conscious that people are looking at you." An audience member visiting Chicago for the first time asked Winfrey to recommend her favorite restaurant in the area. Surprisingly, she replied that she no longer goes out to eat, to avoid the scene that it would cause when people spotted her in public. Instead, she spends most of her free time at her secluded 160-acre farm in Indiana with her friend Gayle King or her long-time companion, Stedman Graham.

Graham, the CEO of a marketing company, is an independent businessman who writes inspirational and leadership books. Winfrey calls him "Steddy" because she says he is her rock. The two were engaged in 1993, but decided to postpone the wedding because the date coincided with the release of Winfrey's autobiography. According to her, the subject has not come up since then. (Ironically, she decided not to release her autobiography after all, saying that she is still a work in progress.) Still, their relationship remains strong. "Stedman and I have a great relationship that allows me to be me in the fullest sense," she explains, "with no expectations of wifedom and all that would mean." When people ask about a wedding date, she says matter of factly, "Neither of us is ready to get married and when we are, we'll get married."

Motherhood is a different story. When Winfrey was thirty-nine, a reporter asked if she felt her biological clock ticking. She responded, "Ticking! It's a gong. I hear it everyday." A couple of years later, her best friend, King, asked her the same question. Her response was very different: "Not a tick, not a tock." After Winfrey turned fifty, her answer was more definitive. "I don't think that's for me," she said, before adding that she has 50,000 children in South Africa who call her mother.

Winfrey says that she is one of the most blessed people in the world because she is paid so handsomely to do a job she loves. She has the wisdom to know that wealth and privilege are accompanied by the responsibility to help others reach their full potential. To that end, she says, "I will continue to use my voice and my life as a catalyst for change, inspiring and encouraging people to help make a difference in the lives of others." Her compassion for people leads her to encourage them to live their best life and to live it with passion.

What the future holds for Oprah Winfrey is unclear, but there is no doubt that she will continue to do great things for her fellow human beings. Like a fine wine, she seems to get better with age. "I'm just getting started," Winfrey says. "If you're open to the possibilities, your life gets grander, bigger, bolder!"

Mike Krzyzewski

Leadership

In June 2004, the Los Angeles Lakers began courting Mike Krzyzewski, the legendary "Coach K" of Duke University, to become their next head coach. This wasn't the first time a professional basketball team had attempted to lure Coach K from Duke—he turned down offers from the Boston Celtics in 1990 and the Miami Heat in 1994—but this was the first time he seemed to express any real interest in making the move. To entice him into taking one of the most prestigious jobs in professional sports, the Lakers were offering Coach K a contract reportedly worth $40 million. He informed Duke's athletic director and president that he would be taking a closer look at the offer, prompting Duke University to acknowledge the swirling rumors in a statement to the media. Shortly thereafter, Mitch Kupchak, general manager of the Lakers, flew to Durham, North Carolina, to meet with Coach K at his home.

The story was quickly becoming one of the biggest news events of the year. Coach K was about to enter his twenty-fifth season at Duke University. In the previous twenty-four years, he had led the Blue Devils to three national championships, ten Final Four appearances, and ten Atlantic Coast Conference (ACC) regular season championships. Because of his outstanding leadership, Coach K had received National Coach of the Year honors twelve times. In 2001 Duke University extended him a lifetime contract and even named the court at Cameron Indoor Stadium "Coach K Court." Students regularly wait up to eight weeks for tickets outside the stadium in an area they fondly call "Krzyzewskiville." It is widely known that Coach K is loved and respected by Duke sports fans everywhere. When word got out that he was seriously considering an offer to move to pro basketball, many students and alumni pleaded with him to stay at Duke.

One of those students was junior Andrew Humphries, a biology major. He sent Coach K a six-page e-mail message. In it he wrote, "We get to Duke and we realize you are our coach. Not just the coach of our team, but you are also our coach.... I was on your team, because I was your sixth man and you were my coach." Humphries ended his message with this plea: "Please still be my coach." Less than a week later, Coach K announced his decision to remain at Duke. When asked why he decided to stay, Coach K surprised many by citing the e-mail message from Andrew Humphries as one of his primary reasons. The coach said it had moved him to tears and reinforced the connection he feels with players, students, and everyone associated with Duke. "That's the type of relationship that has made this place just different, where it's not just been our [the coaches and players'] team," he explained at a press conference. "It's been OUR team, with everybody involved." In the end, all the money in the world could not have changed his mind. Coach K knew that he had to follow his heart, and during his twenty-five years as coach of the Blue Devils he has often said, "Duke has always taken up my whole heart."

Many outsiders thought Coach K's rationale for staying at Duke was hokey, even untrue. "He's not really going to base his decision on an emotional plea from a student he never met," was a common refrain. Or, "it's just a publicity stunt," many outsiders said. However, to those familiar with Coach K and his leadership principles, his rationale made perfect sense. In his best-selling book, *Leading with the Heart,* Coach K wrote, "Almost everything in leadership comes back to relationships." He is careful to use plural pronouns such as "we," "our," and "us" instead of "I," "my," and "me." One of his primary goals as a coach is to create a family environment, and his family includes more than just the players—it includes the entire campus community.

Coach K routinely seeks advice from people who might be frequently overlooked by other leaders. He relies on his secretary, the school's sports information director, and the team manager to help him assess the team's strengths and weaknesses and to point out potential problems. His inclusive approach comes from his philosophy that everybody is equal. Simply having the ability to put a basketball through a hoop does not mean that a player is better than someone who cleans the locker room. The person who performs this task at Cameron Indoor Stadium is a man named D.C. Coach K values D.C.'s input and asks him to keep an eye on the guys on the team. On more than one occasion, D.C. has told Coach K about a player struggling with a personal issue or having problems in the classroom. By sharing the leadership responsibilities for the team, Coach K builds a supportive environment and garners respect for everyone associated with the program.

Each fall season the Blue Devils' first practice takes place at 12:01 a.m. on whatever date is designated by the NCAA as the first practice day. Thousands of fans congregate to cheer on the team during their first practice in an annual tradition known as Midnight Madness. In 1997 a photographer was preparing to take a photo of the team at this event. He situated himself in the rafters high above the court to take the team photo. Just before he snapped the picture, Coach K exclaimed, "Wait a minute. Wait a minute. Something's wrong with this picture. Somebody's missing. It's our sixth man." He then invited several thousand students in the stands to join the team on the floor for the official team picture, which still hangs in the Duke locker room. It was Coach K's way of paying tribute to the fans who faithfully support the team each season.

Students at Duke do not have to pay a fee to attend basketball games. In fact, the best seats in the house are reserved for students. There is, however, one catch. Tickets are available to students on a first-come, first-served basis. Given that Cameron Stadium holds only 9,300 fans, and Duke is consistently ranked as one of the best college basketball teams in the country, tickets are in high demand. That means students must wait in line for their tickets. In a tradition unique to Duke, students begin lining up early for each game. In fact, many line up as far in advance as eight weeks before a game! Despite having access to warm, comfortable dorm rooms, eager students choose to live in tents around Cameron Stadium for weeks leading up to certain game days. Up to fifteen people are permitted per tent, but University guidelines require that at least one person must remain in the tent during the day and at least eight must sleep in the tent each night. If these conditions are not met, the tent and all its occupants are sent to the back of the line. The name given to this tent city is Krzyzewskiville. Coach K has been known to order pizza and soft drinks for the students in Krzyzewskiville, and sometimes he just stops by to thank them for their support. Is it any wonder the stadium's student section is referred to as the "Cameron Crazies"?

Before games against Duke's biggest rivals, Coach K often takes time to address the student body. He shares the scouting report with students and gives them assignments to carry out during the game. Most important, he encourages students to root for Duke and not against the opponents. "Be positive," he says to the students. "Remember, you are our sixth man—a part of our team. So you should act responsibly."

The students usually fulfill their end of the bargain. Every game is a sellout and the students remain standing during the entire game. The only time they sit is when the team sits, such as during a timeout or at halftime. Coach K is careful to make very little distinction between the players and the students. They are equal in his eyes and part of the supportive family environment at Duke. Knowing that, it makes sense that Coach K would strongly consider an e-mail message from a student when deciding whether to stay at Duke. That message, and others like it, reminded him that leaving Duke would feel like leaving a family behind.

Mike Krzyzewski's philosophy of valuing family began with his own parents and siblings while growing up in Chicago. He was born on February 13, 1947, into a hardworking Polish family. His father was an elevator operator at a hotel, while his mother cleaned houses for a living. In all the years of his childhood, Coach K says he cannot remember his parents missing a single day of work. The same work ethic was demanded of Mike and his older brother, Bill. Mike never missed a day of school, and as an adult he went fifteen years without missing a single practice at Duke. The Krzyzewski family had very little money, but somehow they managed to put two boys through Catholic school. "I never even thought about us being poor," Coach K remembers, even though the family did not own a house or a car. What they did have at the Krzyzewski household was a lot of love and pride. Coach K says that his parents set a solid foundation for him. In particular, he praises his mother for helping him become the person he is today. In a touching tribute to her, he once wrote, "When people ask me where I learned commitment, I tell them I learned it from you. When they ask me about unconditional support, I learned it from you. Not being afraid to fail? From you."

In high school, Mike was a solid point guard for the basketball team and was offered an opportunity to play for Coach Bob Knight at West Point, the service academy for the U.S. Army. From Coach Knight he learned about preparation, organization, and the Xs and Os of basketball. "Bob Knight had a big influence on me," he says. "He's a brilliant man, an outstanding coach." When Mike's father died unexpectedly during his senior year at West Point, Coach Knight attended the funeral and mourned alongside his family for several days.

West Point demanded excellence from each student. Krzyzewski seemed to thrive in such a challenging environment. He understood that every cadet essentially majors in leadership during his or her four years at West Point. The school endorses a strict honor code that reads, "A cadet will not lie, cheat or steal—or tolerate those who do." A cadet was only allowed to respond to a question with one of three responses: "Yes, sir," "No, sir," or "No excuse, sir." West Point reinforced values such as discipline, honor and honesty—traits that are now an integral part of Coach K's leadership philosophy at Duke.

After graduation, Krzyzewski was commissioned as an officer and served in the Army from 1969 to 1974. After leaving the military, he served a short stint as Bob Knight's graduate assistant at Indiana University. In 1975, based on a strong recommendation from Coach Knight and a stellar interview, Krzyzewski was named the head coach at West Point. In five years at the helm, he compiled a modest record of 73-59. This record and his strong leadership qualities were enough to turn a few heads at Duke University. On May 4, 1980, Krzyzewski became the head basketball coach at Duke.

Mike Krzyzewski came to be called Coach K because of the difficulty many people had in pronouncing his name (sha-shef´-ski). The name Coach K is now commonly associated with words such as respect, tradition, excellence, and integrity. However, Krzyzewski didn't really become Coach K until his fourth season at Duke. In his first three years, the Blue Devils managed to win only thirty-eight games and endured two losing seasons. Critics launched relentless attacks, and many prominent Duke athletic boosters wanted to fire the unknown coach with the unpronounceable name.

However, Coach K continued to believe in himself and stuck to his core principles. He knew that a coach is only as good as his players and staff, so his first objective was to surround himself with assistant coaches, staff, and players with outstanding character. Of recruiting players, he says, "We search for good kids with strong character—not necessarily kids with great talent who can play, but great individuals who are willing to be part of a team and are coachable." No matter how much talent a player has, Coach K will not offer him a scholarship if he is disrespectful or rude. Coach K pays close attention to the way a recruit demonstrates respect for his parents. He freely admits, "If a young man rolls his eyes when his mother asks me a question, I'm not sure I'm going to offer him a scholarship." He's been around enough to know that if a student has not learned to respect authority at home, he is not likely to respect other authority figures when he gets to college.

Once Coach K has assembled his staff and players, he works hard to establish a group identity. He does this by communicating in a direct and honest manner. One of the first statements he makes to his players each year reflects his straightforward approach. "We have only one rule here," he says. "Don't do anything that's detrimental to yourself. Because if it's detrimental to you, it'll be detrimental to our program and to Duke University." He also makes sure that each player understands his "fair, but not equal" policy. Coach K refuses to make promises about which players will be in the starting lineup and who gets playing time. Each player has the opportunity to earn playing time based on merit and performance. To promise playing time to any one player, the coach knows, would be detrimental to the entire team. This policy builds trust because team members know that Coach K does not play favorites.

Another facet of Coach K's leadership style is that he likes to keep things simple. He initiates the following handshake deal with each player: "I'm going to give you 100 percent. In return, I expect you to graduate." He does not take the term "student-athlete" lightly. Coach K's main objective is to help his student-athletes walk away from Duke with a college diploma. To reinforce this focus on academics, he stresses the importance of time management. Players are expected to maintain a balance between school and basketball. Each player receives a personal date book and is encouraged to map out the entire semester in advance, paying special attention to important exams and due dates for class projects. Finally, Coach K stresses academic integrity. He makes it clear that the worst thing a student-athlete can do is cheat.

One way that Coach K builds team unity is by creating shared goals. Because each team is unique, each team sets unique goals. These shared goals do not have anything to do with winning a specific number of games. Coach K believes it is much more important to set a standard of excellence. "My hunger is not for success, it is for excellence," he explains. "Because when you attain excellence, success just naturally follows." In other words, winning games and championships is a byproduct of striving to do your best every single day. Given Duke's impressive record, people are often surprised that Coach K is not consumed with winning and losing. In fact, after losing

Coach Mike Krzyzewski coaches his team to a hard-fought victory.
Photo courtesy of Duke University.

the 1999 National Championship game to Connecticut, he said, "Losing a basketball game could never break my heart." If every Division 1A school set a goal of winning the national championship, only one team would be successful each year. Instead Coach K focuses on urging his players to improve every day and play to their potential. "If I teach them well, winning games will be a natural result," he said. "If my goal had to be only winning games, I wouldn't be a coach."

To further enhance team unity, Coach K fosters a supportive environment among teammates. At the beginning of the season, he hands out a list with everyone's phone number and encourages players to carry it with them at all times. "Whenever you're in harm's way, make a call. If it's two o'clock in the morning and you're in trouble, someone on this card will help you." He also follows up this encouragement with a word to the wise. "When there's a chance to make a mistake, remember that you're part of our family. And remember that whatever happens to you, happens to us." Statements like this build team pride and foster personal responsibility.

Building supportive relationships based on respect takes time. However, once those relationships are in place, Coach K does not hesitate to give honest feedback to his players. As a coach, nothing is more important than being able to communicate openly and honestly with a player at a given moment. "Fellas, I am the truth," he says. "At any time, I can and will tell you where you stand and how you're doing. I'll tell you what you're doing right and I'll tell you when you're screwing up." If he is successful in establishing a trusting environment, players respond positively to his direct approach. Coach K reminds us that leadership isn't just about "I love you" and "Let's hold hands and skip." Sometimes it requires statements like, "Get your rear in gear" and "What the hell are you doing?" As you might expect from a West Point graduate, discipline is an essential part of his success. Coach K says he doesn't understand how discipline has come to have such a negative connotation. "Discipline is doing what you are supposed to do in the best possible manner at the time you are supposed to do it," he says. "And that's not such a bad thing." He holds his players to the highest standards and is very demanding. In the organized chaos that is basketball, a leader needs to get his players to perform at a moment's notice.

One such moment occurred during the 1992 regional finals against Kentucky. The winner of the game would advance to the Final Four, the pinnacle of college basketball. The game was quickly turning into an epoch match. At the end of regulation, the score was tied at 93. Both teams played a hard-fought overtime, with the lead changing hands several times. With 7.8 seconds remaining on the clock, Duke had a one-point lead at 102-101. Kentucky's legendary coach, Rick Pitino, called a timeout and devised a play that would put Kentucky back into the lead. The strategy worked, and Kentucky took a 103-102 lead with 2.1 seconds remaining.

At that moment you could almost see the wind go out of the Duke players. They were dazed and doubting their chances of winning. The truth is, everybody was. Everybody that is, except Coach K. He quickly called a timeout and summoned his players to the bench. He didn't like the defeated look in their eyes and instantly knew he had to convince them to believe in their ability to prevail. He looked directly into their eyes and said forcefully, "We're going to win! We're going to win!" Once Coach K had their attention, he drew up the play that would win the game. With courage and conviction, he turned to Grant Hill and said, "Grant, we need a three-quarter pass. Grant, can you make the pass?" Hill replied, "Yeah, Coach. I can do it." Coach K then turned to Christian Laettner and said, "Christian, you're going to flash from the left corner to the top of the key. Christian, can you catch it?" Laettner nodded affirmatively. Coach K reminded Laettner that the clock would not start until he touched the ball, so he had 2.1 seconds to make his move. He looked into everybody's eyes once again and said, "We're going to win!"

What happened next is legendary. Hollywood couldn't have written a better script. When Laettner caught the miraculous pass from Hill, he dribbled the ball twice, turned, jumped, and as time expired, the ball swished through the net. Most college basketball fans simply refer to this play as "the shot." Some people say Duke was lucky. However, Coach K knows better. He says, "I think luck favors teams who trust one another." Because Coach K developed trusting relationships, instilled discipline, and inspired confidence in his players, he could count on them to respond when it mattered most. With a lesser coach, it is safe to say that Duke would not have won that game or have gone on to win their second national championship.

Also indicative of Coach K's leadership style was his reaction after the final buzzer sounded against Kentucky. Instead of getting caught up in the hysteria that immediately erupted, he instinctively knew that he had another job to do. He ran over to the Kentucky player situated closest to him. He wrapped his arms around Richie Farmer and tried to console him. In victory and defeat, Coach K never fails to act with class and dignity.

No team has been able to match Duke's consistent level of success under the leadership of Coach K. His simple formula of preparation, communication, hard work, practice, and focus has built a dynasty at Duke. There is little doubt that he is the driving force behind the reputation Duke basketball has enjoyed for the last quarter century. Former player Christian Laettner agrees. "Coach K has been the one constant excellent thing behind Duke basketball," he says. In a sports world that regularly shows signs of moral decay, Coach K is a shining example of dignity and honesty. He runs a clean program and talks at length about tradition, pride, and character. It is not surprising that seven of his former assistant coaches have gone on to become successful head coaches at other Division I universities.

For all of these reasons, other college coaches have a great deal of respect for Coach K. Coach Roy Williams of the University of North Carolina once said, "He's truly one of the greats; there's no question about that. His consistency speaks for itself." Coach Gene Keady of Purdue added, "He's contributed a great deal to our game and truly cares about the sport of basketball at the collegiate level. He runs a top-rated program the right way and his kids always play hard and with integrity. It doesn't get much better than Mike Krzyzewski." Jeff Capel, one of Coach K's assistants who has gone on to coach his own team, said this about his former mentor: "He is a man of outstanding character and a father figure to many that have played for him."

With his strong character and leadership skills, Coach K has been equally successful off the court. In 2004 he and his wife, Mickie, celebrated their thirty-fifth wedding anniversary. Together they have raised three wonderful daughters. Coach K also gives generously of his time to the community. He serves as chairman of the Duke Children's Miracle Network Telethon and has helped to raise millions of dollars for the Jimmy V Foundation, named in honor of his former colleague at North Carolina State University. To honor his mother, he founded the Emily Krzyzewski Family Center, which provides services to needy families in Durham. The entire Krzyzewski family is involved in campaigns to keep kids in school and off drugs. A few years ago Coach K became so involved in charities, fundraisers, and worthy causes, that he had to cut back to maintain a healthy balance in his life—something he knows is critical to maintaining his effectiveness as a leader.

Coach K's leadership principles are not just applicable to coaching. Business leaders and CEOs from across the country have applied his strategies in corporate America. Several university professors require students to read his book on leadership to prepare them for success in school and the business world. Despite his widespread popularity, Coach K thinks of himself as just a college coach committed to making a positive impact on Duke's student-athletes. Many fans believe that if he keeps up his present pace, he will retire with more wins than any other coach at the Division I level. He already has more NCAA tournament wins than any other coach in history. Longtime ESPN basketball analyst Dick Vitale had this to say about Coach K: "Mike Krzyzewski has become the most dominant coaching force in all of college basketball. The numbers don't shock me and they will continue to grow, as he is a complete leader in every way. He is a master motivator, teacher, communicator, and genuine solid gold Hall of Famer."

There are several qualities that make Coach K an outstanding leader and set him apart from his peers. First, Coach K is willing to take responsibility for his actions. He regularly admits his mistakes, apologizes for his errors, and takes corrective steps to make things right. Coach K once said, "When you are the CEO of your own company, I want you to remember that you should still clean up your own mess." As the leader of his team, he nurtures caring relationships and creates a family environment on the team and at the university. The basketball family needs rebuilding each year as some players graduate or move on to the pros, yet he is able to successfully lead the team through that difficult transition every time. Because Coach K puts such a strong emphasis on relationships, he has the uncanny ability to read his players and know whether they need a pat on the back or a kick in the rear. His communication style is direct and honest, leaving little room for misunderstanding. He is also wise enough to know that he can always improve. With a continued emphasis on getting better, he is constantly learning new strategies to make him a better leader. And finally, Coach K has the courage to stick to his convictions. He once said, "Courage gives a leader the ability to stand straight and not sway no matter which way the wind blows." Because of his courage, he is able to make tough decisions in a split second and live with the outcome—win, lose, or draw.

While most of you will never become a college basketball coach, all of you will take on leadership responsibilities at some point in your life. Simply becoming a parent will put you in a leadership position. Some of you will be responsible for leading employees at work, while others will take on leadership roles in the community. Even in high school, coaches expect players to become leaders on and off the field. Teachers want students to lead by example—study hard, follow the rules, and help other students when they need it. Remember that when you're with a group of friends and are confronted with a real-life ethical dilemma, you can show courage by doing the right thing. In all of these situations, it is better to lead by virtue than follow the crowd.

Character

What They All Have in Common

Perhaps the best way to define character is to visualize it as the centerpiece of all the specific traits discussed in this book. The figure located on the opposite page helps the reader understand this imagery. Much like the human heart, which can only pump when all the other essential organs work in harmony, a person can only have good character when the necessary traits come together to surround it. In other words, to have good character, you must first be honest, respectful, responsible, loyal, and so on. If a person fails to demonstrate a particular character trait, we call that a character flaw, and that person must work hard to improve in this area.

Using this definition, we can say Arthur Ashe was a man of great character because he demonstrated so many of these essential character traits. He was courageous in the face of discrimination, compassionate toward others, took responsibility for himself, showed tremendous integrity throughout his life, and persevered despite tremendous obstacles. The same argument can be made for each person profiled in this book. Each individual exemplifies a particular character trait, but each person also demonstrates many other aspects of strong character. That is why the title of this book is *Role Models: Examples of Character & Leadership*. All of the individuals included in this book are worthy of our respect, and their lives should inspire us to become better people.

The previous seventeen chapters described the lives of seventeen role models. Each chapter helps us to understand what set that person apart and made him or her unique. In focusing on one particular person, it is easy to see what he or she did to demonstrate that particular character trait. This final chapter will document what these seventeen individuals had in common—all are persons of strong character. While it is impossible to say that every person demonstrates every character trait, it is helpful to consider what they have in common. If we can understand what inspired these role models to greatness, perhaps we can match their examples. Very few of us will become a movie star, a professional athlete, or a CEO of a major corporation, but we can all demonstrate strong character in our professional and personal lives. When we do that, we become leaders and role models for the next generation.

Goals

In order to become successful, one must set goals. Whatever ambition you have for the future, goals will help you reach your objectives. As a boy, Tiger Woods set a long-term goal of becoming the best golfer of all time. He also set short-term goals to guide his journey. He had a list of Jack Nicklaus' achievements and used that as a blueprint. For example, Nicklaus broke seventy for the first time when he was thirteen, so Tiger set a goal to break seventy when he was twelve—and he did. Now, as an adult, he has set a goal of winning nineteen majors, one more than Nicklaus won in his distinguished career. This goal keeps Tiger going, even when he finds himself in an occasional slump.

After Christopher Reeve broke his neck and became a quadriplegic, he set a long-term goal to walk again. In order to accomplish this goal, he set smaller, daily goals in physical therapy and worked tirelessly to breathe without a ventilator. He said that if a cure for paralysis were found, he wanted his body to be prepared to walk again. He also gave speeches and raised money so that researchers could have the resources to work toward a cure. Unfortunately, Reeve died before he was able to walk again, but his efforts may have laid the foundation for others with similar injuries to walk in the future.

When Jesse Ventura discovered that politicians in his community were not acting on behalf of the citizens who had elected them, he set a goal of becoming mayor of Brooklyn Park, Minnesota. When he learned that state politicians planned to keep $4 billion of taxpayers' money, he set a goal to become the next governor of Minnesota.

Calculated Risks

Many people tend to stick with the same old routine and never realize their full potential. They live their lives in fear of the unknown, always choosing the safest option. One of the keys to becoming successful is to take calculated risks in life. This does not mean you have to risk life and limb, but it does mean that sometimes you have to be willing to risk a little to get a lot. When he was just sixteen years old, Booker T. Washington traveled several hundred miles—mostly on foot—just for the chance to get an education. He didn't even know if Hampton Institute would admit him, but he was determined to take the risk. Later in life, he was invited to serve as principal of Tuskegee Institute. Despite the fact that the school did not have a building or even any teachers, he accepted the position. Before he died, the school had over 100 buildings and 200 faculty members.

Oprah Winfrey has taken calculated risks her entire life. When *The Oprah Winfrey Show* went into syndication across the country, she was earning millions of dollars. She could have lived happily on this salary for the rest of her life. However, in a savvy business move, she started her own business. She bought the rights to her show, purchased her own studio, and took on the responsibility of paying the staff herself. She made a huge investment up front for a big payoff down the road. It is largely due to that decision that she became the first female African-American billionaire in the world.

Amelia Earhart routinely took risks in the air, and in the process she set many flying records. She became the first woman to fly across the Atlantic Ocean, and she set out to be the first person to fly around the world at the equator. Although she did not survive that bold attempt, she understood the risks and believed in what she was doing. In a farewell letter to her husband, she wrote, "Please know I am quite aware of the hazards. I want to do it because I want to do it. Women must try to do things as men have tried. When they fail, their failure must be but a challenge to others."

Humility

When Cal Ripken Jr. broke Lou Gehrig's record for most consecutive games played, Ripken deflected much of the resulting notoriety and fame. When asked about his amazing accomplishment, he said, "All I ever wanted to do was play well and play every day." Then instead of talking about himself, he acknowledged his teammates and family. And instead of drawing attention to his own abilities, he made sure to pay homage to the great Lou Gehrig. People respect that kind of humility. No one wants to hear others sing their own praises, even if they have accomplished great things.

Pat Tillman also recognized the importance of humility. When he gave up a professional football contract worth $3.5 million to enlist in the Army, he did so quietly. Members of the media were not alerted and no public statements were issued. When Tillman and his brother received the Arthur Ashe Courage Award, they politely declined to attend the ESPY ceremony to receive the award. Tillman did not want to do anything to call attention to himself. He did not think he deserved special recognition for making a career change. In his eyes, if the media singled him out, they would be discounting the sacrifice of thousands of other soldiers who were also bravely serving their country in the military.

Bob Hope was the same way. He risked his life countless times just to show his appreciation to the men and women of the U.S. military. Whenever he was praised for his service, he shrugged it off and instead talked about the soldiers who were fighting and dying for their country.

Positive Attitude

Regardless of what life threw at them, the people included in this book maintained a positive outlook on life. They did not let their challenges and problems get them down. They did not whine or complain about how life is unfair. Life was certainly not fair to Helen Keller. As the result of a high fever during her early childhood, she lost the ability to see and hear. Yet she never focused on what she didn't have. Because of her positive outlook on life, she was able to accomplish unbelievable feats. She learned to communicate, graduated from college, traveled the world, and wrote thirteen books in her lifetime.

The same can be said for Mattie Stepanek. Life dealt him a tragic hand. He lost three siblings to muscular dystrophy before learning that he too suffered from the deadly disease. Mattie required the assistance of a wheelchair and a ventilator. He spent most of his abbreviated life fighting death. However, this little boy remained the eternal optimist. He dedicated much of his time to helping others, and he wrote five best-selling poetry books. The world came to love Mattie because he lived every day to the fullest and remained hopeful about the future.

Similarly, Nancy Reagan was dealt a devastating blow in her lifetime. Just when she and President Reagan were entering the twilight of their lives, he was diagnosed with Alzheimer's disease. She refused to let the world pity either of them, however. She was honest about the hardship her husband's illness put on her and their marriage, but she chose to focus on the positive memories she was left with when he died.

Integrity

A person with integrity has developed a value system from within that is based on honesty, fairness, and ethical principles. Dwight Eisenhower had a sense of integrity that guided him as he made one difficult decision after another. He might not have always made the right decision, but his decision making process was always guided by ethical principles. Perhaps that is all we can ever ask of a general leading his troops into battle or a president representing America's best interest in the world. Perhaps that's all we can ask of any person.

Mike Krzyzewski is also a man of great integrity. When confronted with an offer to leave Duke University to become the coach of the Los Angeles Lakers, he was not swayed by the $40 million contract on the table. He let his principles guide his decision. In the end, loyalty and commitment won out over the almighty dollar. Coach K continues to run an admirable basketball program; his players graduate from college and win with class.

Another shining example of integrity is Sherron Watkins. In the midst of rampant fraud at Enron, she was the only person brave enough to report the unethical practices to the company CEO. Likewise, she is one of a handful of people to go before the U.S. Congress and answer questions with openness and honesty. For this, members of Congress praised her. Representative Cliff Stearns said, "I believe that employees such as yourself, in no small measure, contribute to the integrity of our commercial system by insisting that all participants play by the rules."

Working-Class Families

Nearly every person in this book came from a working-class family that had little money. Perhaps this is why each one understood the importance of traits such as discipline, hard work, and perseverance. While their parents may have been short on money, they provided plenty of love, support, and moral guidance. No one in this book had life handed to him or her on a silver platter. They had to go out and make their own way in the world. And make it they did. From meager beginnings, they became talk show hosts, actors, corporate executives, pilots, athletes, coaches, governors, and presidents. That is what makes America great—the possibilities are endless. Just like Dwight Eisenhower's mother told him, "Opportunity is all about you. Reach out and take it."

Giving Back

All of the people included in this book gave generously of their time, energy, and resources. They did so in different ways, but they all gave back to society. Tiger Woods, Arthur Ashe, Christopher Reeve, Mike Krzyzewski, and Cal Ripken Jr. started foundations to help others. Oprah Winfrey has donated over $175 million to charities and has served as a mentor for young girls from low-income families. Martin Luther King Jr. dedicated his life to ending segregation and discrimination. Helen Keller gave freely of her time to help the blind. Mattie Stepanek served as national ambassador for the Muscular Dystrophy Association and helped raise money to find a cure for the disease. Throughout his lifetime, Bob Hope donated his time to entertain the troops overseas. Dwight Eisenhower, Jesse Ventura, and Pat Tillman chose to serve their country in the military.

By giving so much of themselves, all of these role models leave behind a legacy of compassion. It is not always necessary to donate millions of dollars or sacrifice your life for a noble cause. We can all find people who are in needy circumstances and could benefit from the gift of our time, possessions, or money. Giving back is a choice, and we all can do our small part to make the world a better place.

Learning from Mistakes

The other common attribute that everyone in this book shares is fallibility. Each of these role models is human and made his or her fair share of mistakes. However, what separates the people in this book from others with weaker character is that these men and women learned from their mistakes and went on to make better decisions. As a child, Dwight Eisenhower had a terrible temper, but he learned to control it as he matured. As an adult, he was known for his ability to stay calm during a crisis. When Tiger Woods was a rookie on the PGA, he skipped an event that was to be held in his honor. He received harsh criticism for this poor decision. To make up for it, he sent handwritten letters of apology to each person invited to the event, reimbursed the tournament sponsors for the cost of the dinner, and requested that it be rescheduled for a later date.

After being sexually abused as a child, Oprah Winfrey became a sexually promiscuous teenager. At the age of fourteen she gave birth to a child who soon died. Oprah's father told her that she had been given a second chance at life and encouraged her to make good on it. She turned her life around, applied herself, and became a successful talk show host, businesswoman, and actress.

Looking up to Role Models

When Amelia Earhart was a young girl, she kept a scrapbook of female role models who had achieved greatness in male-dominated fields. These role models inspired her to learn to fly. Martin Luther King Jr. read about prominent African Americans who came before him such as Booker T. Washington, Harriet Tubman, Frederick Douglass, and Jesse Owens. These people inspired him to do something great with his own life. The same could be said for Tiger Woods. He studied golf's greatest players and used them as a guide to better his own play. Others like Cal Ripken Jr. and Mike Krzyzewski said that their parents were their role models. Helen Keller and Oprah Winfrey credited schoolteachers as their role models.

Conclusion

The main reason I decided to write this book was to provide young people with positive role models. I had become discouraged with the types of individuals serving as role models for our youth today. This book is filled with people who have done remarkable things while exhibiting strong character. Some of these individuals are historical figures whose accomplishments have stood the test of time, while others are living examples of what is possible. Regardless of when they were born or what profession they chose, we should study their lives, applaud them, and strive to emulate their behavior and high level of achievement.

Sir Isaac Newton once said, "If I have seen further than others, it is by standing on the shoulders of giants." My hope is that you have found a few "giants" in this book worthy of being called your role models. Perhaps they will inspire you to be a better person and to do great things with your life. Also, I hope this book will inspire you to read about and emulate other strong role models in society. There are only seventeen people in this book, yet one could argue that thousands of others could have been included. Seek them out, learn from them, and follow in their footsteps. Who knows, if you integrate enough of these character traits into your own life, you too might be considered a role model to others.

Bibliography

Chapter 1. Mattie Stepanek

Dart, Bob. "13-year-old poet, activist remembered as 'an angel.'" *The Palm Beach Post*, June 29, 2004.

Edwards, Bob. "Profile: Eleven-year-old Mattie Stepanek's poetry." *Morning Edition*, NPR, December 28, 2001.

Hume, Brit, and Juan Williams. "Interview with Mattie and Jeni Stepanek." *Special Report with Brit Hume*, Fox News Network, December 25, 2002.

Manning, Stephen. "Mattie Stepanek, poet, advocate, dies." AP Online, June 23, 2004.

Manning, Stephen. "Former President Carter, mourners bury beloved young-poet." AP Worldstream, June 29, 2004.

Mattie Stepanek's Personal Website. "About Mattie Stepanek." http://www.mattieonline.com.

Muscular Dystrophy Association. "Eulogies from Jimmy Carter and Oprah Winfrey." http://www.mdausa.org.

The My Hero Project. "Poet Heroes." http://www.myhero.com.

PR Newswire. "Fire fighters say farewell to Mattie Stepanek: 13-year-old MDA National goodwill ambassador was great inspiration to America's bravest." June 23, 2004.

Sachs, Andrea. "Hot Property: Mattie Stepanek's deadly illness hasn't stopped him from writing his best-selling poetry books." *Teen People*, May 1, 2002.

Stepanek, Mattie. *Heartsongs*. New York: VSP Books, 2001.

Waters, Jen. "Spirit Soars in Rockville: 12-year-old lives full life in wheelchair." *The Washington Times*, January 21, 2003.

Wilson, Craig. "Boy's poetry from the heart inspires others to hope." *USA Today*, December 13, 2001.

Winfrey, Oprah. "What I Know for Sure." *O Magazine*, November 1, 2002.

Chapter 2. Tiger Woods

Callahan, Tom. *In Search of Tiger: A Journey Through Golf with Tiger Woods*. New York: Crown Publishers, 2003.

Official Site for Tiger Woods. "About Tiger: Biography." http://www.tigerwoods.com.

The Official Site of Jack Nicklaus. "Facts and Figures." http://http://nicklaus.com.

Strege, John. *Tiger: A Biography of Tiger Woods*. New York: Broadway Books, 1997.

Tiger Woods Foundation. "Tiger's Letter." http://www.twfound.org.

Woods, Earl with Pete McDaniel. *Training A Tiger: A Father's Guide to Raising A Winner in Both Golf and Life*. New York: HarperCollins, 1997.

Chapter 3. Booker T. Washington

Links to the Past: National Park Service Cultural Resources. "Biography of Booker T. Washington." http://www.cr.nps.gov.

Tuskegee University. "History of Tuskegee University." http://www.tuskegee.edu.

Washington, Booker T. *Up From Slavery*. New York: Penguin Books, 1986 (originally published in 1901).

Chapter 4. Dwight Eisenhower

Ambrose, Stephen E. *Eisenhower: Soldier and President*. New York: Simon & Schuster, 1990.

Ambrose, Stephen E. *D-Day: The Climactic Battle of World War II*. New York: Simon & Schuster, 1994.

Chapter 5. Sherron Watkins

About.com. "Late-Night Jokes About the Enron Scandal." http://politicalhumor.about.com.

Ackman, Dan. "Sherron Watkins Had Whistle, But Blew It." *Forbes*, February 14, 2002.

American Patriot Friends Network. "Text of Sherron Watkins' Testimony at House Hearing on Enron." http://www.apfn.org, February 14, 2002.

CourtTV.com: The Investigation Channel. "Enron Employees to get at least $66.5 million in settlement." http://www.courttv.com.

Frey, Jennifer. "Sherron Watkins: Woman Who Saw Red." *The Washington Post,* January 25, 2002.

Investopedia.com. "The Biggest Stock Scams of All Time." http://www.investopedia.com.

LeClaire, Jennifer. "Limits of a Whistle-Blower Culture." *The Christian Science Monitor,* http://www.csmonitor.com, October 21, 2002.

Morse, Jodie, and Amanda Bower. "Persons of the Year 2002: Party Crasher. *Time,* December 22, 2002.

Minnesota Treasury Management Association. "Sherron Watkins." http://www.mtma.com,

Paulsen, Steve. "Workers Lose Jobs, Health Care and Savings at Enron." World Socialist Web Site, http://www.wsws.org, January 14, 2002.

Pellegrini, Frank. "Person of the Week: 'Enron Whistleblower' Sherron Watkins." http://www.time.com, January 18, 2002.

Swartz, Mimi with Sherron Watkins. *Power Failure: The Inside Story of the Collapse of Enron.* New York: Doubleday, 2003.

Time.com. "Persons of the Year 2002: The Interview." http://www.time.com, December 22, 2002.

Chapter 6. Jesse Ventura

All Science Fair Projects. "Post-Gubernatorial Life." http://www.all-science-fair-projects.com.

Brainy Dictionary. "Definition of Integrity." http://www.brainydictionary.com.

Frank, Stephen I., and Steven C. Wagner. *We Shocked the World: A Case Study of Jesse Ventura's Election as Governor of Minnesota.* Orlando, Florida: Harcourt College Publishers, 2001.

GoodCharacter.com. "Integrity Lesson Plan." http://www.goodcharacter.com.

Harvard University Institute of Politics. "Jesse Ventura." http://www.iop.harvard.edu.

Ventura, Jesse. *I Ain't Got Time To Bleed.* New York: Signet, 1999.

Ventura, Jesse, with Julie Mooney. *Do I Stand Alone? Going to the Mat Against Political Pawns and Media Jackals.* New York: Pocket Books, 2000.

Chapter 7. Amelia Earhart

123HelpMe.com. "To Kill a Mockingbird—Courage," http://www.123helpme.com.

Ascribe Higher Education New Service. "Purdue University libraries land rare items for Amelia Earhart Collection." May 2, 2002.

Earhart. Amelia. *20 Hrs., 40 Min. Our Flight in the Friendship.* Washington, D.C.: National Geographic Adventure Classics, 2003 (originally published 1928).

Egan, Erin. "Legends: Amelia Earhart was a courageous pilot and a hero to both women and men." *Sports Illustrated Kids*, December 1, 1994.

Hall, Doug, and Russ Quaglia. "Plant the seeds for mustering courage." *Seattle Post-Intelligencer*, March 1, 1999.

McGuire, Donna. "Researchers work on 3 theories on Amelia Earhart's disappearance." Knight Ridder/Tribune News Service, August 19, 2001.

Michaelson, Mike. "Memory of Amelia Earhart still flies high in Atchinson." *Daily Herald* (Arlington Heights, Illinois), March 24, 2002.

The Official Site of Amelia Earhart. "Biography." http://www.ameliaearhart.com.

Sloate, Susan. Amelia Earhart: *Challenging The Skies.* New York: Fawcett Books, 1990.

Williams, Larry. "Amelia Earhart's epic attempt to fly around the world will be retraced on its 60th anniversary." Knight Ridder/Tribune News Service, February 27, 1997.

Chapter 8. Christopher Reeve

The Battalion Online. "Reeve regains sensation in hands, feet seven years after accident." http://www.thebatt.com.

CBS News.com. "A Recovery Worth of Superman." http://www.cbsnews.com, September 12, 2002.

CBS News.com. "Robin Williams Extols Reeve." http://www.cbsnews.com, October 14, 2004.

Gliatto, Tom, and Samantha Miller, Michelle Tauber, Jason Lynch. "Incredible Journey." *People Magazine*, October 25, 2004.

The Juicy Cerebellum. "A Tribute To Christopher Reeve." http://www.juicycerebellum.com.

Kalb, Claudia and Debra Rosenberg. "Stem Cell Division." *Newsweek*, October 25, 2004.

Reeve, Christopher. *Nothing Is Impossible: Reflections on a New Life*. New York: Ballantine Books, 2002.

Reeve, Christopher. *Still Me*. New York: Random House, 1998.

Superman Homepage. "Superman Profile." http://www.supermanhomepage.com.

Chapter 9. Martin Luther King Jr.

Atlanta Inquirer. "Daily Lessons on the Values and Teachings of Martin Luther King Jr." January 15, 2000.

Davidson, Margaret. *I Have A Dream: The Story of Martin Luther King*. New York: Scholastic Inc., 1986.

Hampson, Rick. "Suspect 'traveled back to roots of black power.'" *USA Today*, March 22, 2000.

Hansen, Liane. "Profile: Dr. Martin Luther King Jr.'s acceptance speech after winning the Nobel Peace Prize in 1964." *NPR's Weekend Edition*, October 14, 2001.

King, Dexter. "Dexter King Discusses Growing Up King." By Tony Cox. *The Tavis Smiley Show*, NPR, April 4, 2003.

Ling, Peter. "We shall overcome: Peter Ling analyses Martin Luther King's involvement with non-violent protest in the USA." *History Review*, March 1, 2003.

Pastan, Amy. *Martin Luther King, Jr.: A Photographic Story of a Life*. New York: DK Publishing, 2004.

Chapter 10. Helen Keller

123Student, Inc. "Biography of Helen Keller." http://www.123student.com.

Garrett, Leslie. *Helen Keller: A Photographic Story of a Life*. New York: DK Publishing, 2004.

Helen Keller Services for the Blind. "Biography." http://www.helenkeller.org.

Keller, Helen. *The Story of My Life*. New York: Bantam Books, 1990 (originally published 1902).

Motivational & Inspirational Corner. "Helen Keller quotations." www.motivational-inspirational-corner.com.

Rich East High School. "Who is Helen Keller?"
http://www.richeast.org.

Schoenberg, Nara. "Helen Keller's story fading out of schools."
Chicago Tribune, August 12, 2003.

Terzian, Phillip. "Reintroducing Helen Keller." Knight
Ridder/Tribune News Service, September 3, 1998.

Chapter 11. Bob Hope

A&E Biography. "Bob Hope." Videotape.

Associated Press. "Celebrities React to Bob Hope's Death." July 28,
2003.

Associated Press. "Hope's Honors Include Peabody Awards, Special
Oscars." AP Worldstream, July 28, 2003.

Associated Press. "Bush Joins Nation in Mourning Bob Hope." AP
Online, July 29, 2003.

Berbeo, Dominic. "Los Angeles Airport's New USO Center Will Be
Named After Bob Hope." Knight Ridder/Tribune Business News,
October 16, 2001.

El Sawy, Nada. "Family Buries Bob Hope After Dawn Funeral," AP
Online, July 31, 2003.

Elber, Lynn. "Entertainer Bob Hope Dies at 100." AP Online, July 28,
2003.

Faith, William Robert. *Bob Hope: A Life In Comedy*. Cambridge,
Massachusetts: Da Capo Press, 1982.

Hope, Bob, and Pete Martin. Have Tux Will Travel: Bob Hope's Own
Story. New York: Simon & Schuster, 1954.

Leigh, Alan. "Timeline Bob Hope 1903–2003." *Hollywood Reporter*,
July 29, 2003.

The Library of Congress. "Bob Hope & American Variety."
http://www.loc.gov.

Morfit, Cameron. "A Golfing Life: Bob Hope 1903–2003."
Sports Illustrated, August 4, 2003.

Nanda, Samantha. "Tributes to Legend That Was Bob Hope."
Evening Telegraph, July 29, 2003.

Stars and Stripes. "100 Years of Bob Hope Presented by Stars &
Stripes." http://www.stripes.com.

Thomas, Bob. "Entertainer Bob Hope Eulogized as Legendary Figure of 20th Century." AP Worldstream, August 27, 2003.

USO, Inc. "The Spirit of Bob Hope Award," http://www.uso.org.

USO, Inc. "The USO Remembers Bob Hope," http://www.uso.org.

USO, Inc. "Bob Hope's USO Tours," http://www.uso.org.

USO, Inc. "Historical Timeline," http://www.uso.org.

USO, Inc. "USO Background," http://www.uso.org.

Chapter 12. Arthur Ashe

Ashe, Arthur and Arnold Rampersad. *Days of Grace*. New York: Alfred A. Knopf Inc., 1993.

Avert.org. "World HIV and AIDS Statistics." http://www.avert.org.

CMG Worldwide. "Arthur Ashe." www.cmgww.com.

CNN.com. "Even after death, Arthur Ashe topples another barrier." http://www.cnn.com, July 11, 1996.

"Arthur Ashe." *Sports Century*, ESPN, 2002.

More, Kenny. "Sportsman of the Year." *Sports Illustrated*, December 21, 1992.

National Institute of Allergy and Infectious Diseases. "HIV/AIDS Statistics." http://www.niaid.nih.gov.

PR Newswire. "Arthur Ashe Commemorative stamp unveiled at US Open." August 28, 2004.

Chapter 13. Pat Tillman

American Battle Monuments Commission. "WWII Casualties." http://www.abmc.gov.

Associated Press. "Tillmans to Receive Espy's Courage Award." AP Online, July 2, 2003.

Emmons, Mark. "Tillman, Who Gave Up NFL for Iraq, Still Humble About Espys." *San Jose Mercury News*, July 15, 2003.

Jeansonne, John. "Driven by His Private Sense of Duty." *Newsday*, April 24, 2004.

Lacayo, Richard. "One For The Team: Pat Tillman—Football Star, Ranger—Did Not Aspire to Heroism. But His Life Defined It." *Time*, May 3, 2004.

National Baseball Hall of Fame and Museum. "1942: When Baseball Went to War."

http://www.baseballhalloffame.org.

Organization of American Historians. "Baseball and World War II." http://www.oah.org.

Rand, Jonathan. *Fields of Honor: The Pat Tillman Story.* New York: Chamberlain Bros., 2004.

Towle, Mike. *I've Got Things To Do With My Life.* Chicago: Triumph Books, 2004.

The Washington Post. "Facing Fine, Plummer Pays Tribute." October 11, 2004.

Chapter 14. Nancy Reagan

Aaron, Lawrence. "Reagan's Last Exit: 'Role of a Lifetime.'" *The Record* (Bergen County, New Jersey), June 16, 2004.

Agence France Presse. "Loyalty to 'Ronnie' Transforms Nancy Reagan's Image From Socialite to Saint." June 10, 2004.

Connelly, Sheryl. "Nancy Reagan Devoted to Her Husband and His Legacy." *New York Daily News,* June 5, 2004.

Davis, Patti. *The Long Goodbye.* New York: Alfred A. Knopf Inc., 2004.

Edwards, Anne. *The Reagans: Portrait of a Marriage.* New York: St. Martin's Griffin, 2003.

Flaim, Denise. "Devoted to Ronnie Over 52 Years, Nancy Reagan Was Her Husband's Admirer, Partner, Promoter, Surrogate and Caregiver." *Newsday,* June 7, 2004.

Flass, Rebecca. "Quiet Suburb Shining as Home of Reagan's Final Resting Place." *Los Angeles Business Journal,* June 21, 2004.

Heyman, J.D., and Champ Clark, Macon Morehouse, Tom Duffy. "Nancy Reagan: A New Chapter." *People Magazine,* June 28, 2004.

Kemper, Bob. "Ronald Reagan: 1911–2004: Funeral Steeped in Protocol, Traditions Spelled Out in Manual." *The Atlanta Journal and Constitution,* June 28, 2004.

Ludtke, Melissa. "Co-Starring at the White House: Nancy Reagan's Clout and Causes Bring New Respect." *Time,* January 14, 1985.

Page, Susan. "Husband's Past Will Shape Nancy Reagan's Future: Friends Say She Will Step Forward to Promote His Legacy." *USA Today,* June 14, 2004.

Plummer, William, and Pamela Warrick, Margery Sellinger. "Endless Love: Once Considered Cold and Controlling, Nancy Reagan Emerges as a Selfless Caregiver." *People Magazine*, March 13, 2000.

Reagan, Nancy. *I Love You, Ronnie: The Letters of Ronald Reagan to Nancy Reagan*. New York: Random House, 2000.

Reagan, Nancy with William Novak. *My Turn: The Memoirs of Nancy Reagan*. New York: Random House, 1989.

Reagan, Ronald. *Ronald Reagan: An American Life*. New York: Pocket Books, 1990.

Schindette, Susan, and Champ Clark, Tom Cunneff, Vicki Sheff-Cahan, Frank Swertlow, Macon Morehouse, Juliet Butler, Tom Duffy. "Journey's End: Actor, President, Husband, Father." *People Magazine*, June 21, 2004.

Thomas, Evan, and Eleanor Clift, Debra Rosenberg, Holly Bailey, Steve Tuttle, Jennifer Ordonez, Deidre Depke. "As the Shadows Fell: The Story of Ronald Reagan's Last Decade is at Once Grim and Tender." *Newsweek*, June 21, 2004.

Chapter 15. Cal Ripken Jr.

Bodley, Hal. "Projects Keep Ripken Busy." *USA Today*, February 15, 2002.

BookRags.com. "Profile of Cal Ripken, Jr." http://www.bookrags.com.

ESPN.com. "MLB—Countdown Begins: Strike Date Set for Aug. 30." http://www.espn.go.com.

ESPN.com. "Cal Ripken, Jr." http://www.espn.go.com.

ESPN.com. "Iron Man Ripken Brought Stability to Shortstop." http://espn.go.com, September 2002

Kurkjian, Tim. "Man of Iron." *Sports Illustrated*, August 7, 1995.

Marantz, Steve. "Iron Clan." *The Sporting News*, December 18, 1995.

The My Hero Project. "Calvin Edwin Ripken Jr." http://www.myhero.com.

Plummer, William. "Man At Work: In an age of prima donnas, steady Cal Ripken breaks baseball's ultimate blue-collar record." *People Magazine*, September 18, 1995.

Ripken, Cal Jr. and Mike Bryan. *The Only Way I Know*. New York: Penguin Books, 1997.

Ripken, Cal Jr. and Mike Bryan. *Cal Ripken, Jr.: My Story*. New York: Dial Books for Young Readers, 1999.

Sports Illustrated. "Sportsman of the Year." http://www.sportsillustrated.com, December 18, 1995.

USA Today. "The Ripken Resume: Numbers Add Up To Greatness." http://www.usatoday.com.

Volunteers of America. " How to Help." http://www.volunteersofamerica.org.

Wiley, Ralph. "A Monumental Streak: In 8 Years, Baltimore's Cal Ripken, Jr. Hasn't Missed A Game." *Sports Illustrated*, June 18, 1990.

Wulf, Steve. "Iron Bird." *Time*, September 11, 1995.

Chapter 16. Oprah Winfrey

Agence France Presse English. "Oprah donates one million dollars for black history center." July 9, 2004.

Agence France Presse English. "Oprah surprises teachers with pre-Thanksgiving day giveaway." November 23, 2004.

Associated Press. "Oprah Winfrey wins Hope Humanitarian award at 54th Emmys." AP Worldstream, September 23, 2002.

Business Week.com. "Online Extra: A Talk with Oprah Winfrey." http://www.businessweek.com, November 29, 2004.

Calio, Jim. "If you knew Oprah like I know Oprah..." *Redbook*, February 1, 1998.

Carlson, Peter. "O is for Oprah, Oozing Oodles of Optimism." *The Washington Post*, April 25, 2000.

Conlin, Michelle, and Lauren Gard, Jessi Hempel, Kate Hazelwood, David Polek, Tony Bianc. "The Top Givers." *Business Week*, November 29, 2004.

Harrington, Ann, and Petra Bartosiewicz. "Who's Up? Who's Down? And is that a new no.1? Yes and seven rising stars hit the list for the first time." *Fortune*, October 18, 2004.

Lowe, Janet. *Oprah Winfrey Speaks*. New York: John Wiley & Sons Inc., 1998.

Miller, Nicholas. "Oprah donates $1 million to school children." *Weekly Journal*, November 11, 1993.

Newsweek. "Oprah on Oprah: Perfectionist. Optimist. Diva." January 8, 2001.

Oprah.com. "Oprah's Angel Network." http://www.oprah.com.

Perkins, Ken Parish. "Oprah Winfrey still wonders how she became the queen of all media." Knight Ridder/Tribune News Service, May 5, 2004.

Randolph, Laura B. "Oprah opens up about her weight, her wedding and why she withheld the book." *Ebony*, October 1, 1993.

Sawyer, Diane, and Barbara Walters. "People Who Have The Power to Make You Look at Your Own Life." *20/20*, ABC, October 25, 1998.

Sellers, Patricia. "The Business of Being Oprah." *Fortune*, April 1, 2002.

Tauber, Michelle. "Prime Time of Her Life: Oprah at 50." *People Magazine*, February 2, 2004.

Winfrey, Oprah, and Kelly Williams. "Drive, she said: Revved up for her 19th season, Oprah Winfrey gives her audience whiplash by handing out 276 new cars." *People Magazine*, September 27, 2004.

Zoglin, Richard. "Lady with a calling." *Time*, August 8, 1988

Chapter 17. Coach K

Barnhouse, Wendell. "Coach K is the force behind Duke's success." Knight Ridder/Tribune News Service, October 3, 2001.

Beard, Aaron. "Student E-Mail Touches Duke's Krzyzewski." AP Online, July 6, 2004.

Cole, Bill. "The 700 Club." *The Winston-Salem Journal*, December 12, 2004.

Docie, Michael. "Krzyzewski returns to Duke bench with new outlook on life and coaching." *Newsday*, November 26, 1995.

Duke University. " Duke Athletics." http://www.duke.edu.

GoDuke.com: The Official Site of Duke University Athletics. "Success On and Off the Court." http://www.goduke.collegesports.com.

GoDuke.com: The Official Site of Duke University Athletics. "Duke Dedicates Court to Mike Krzyzewski." http://www.goduke.collegesports.com.

Hannon, Kerry. "Coach K hits basics of leadership: simple message in mantra for success." *USA Today*, April 17, 2000.

Krzyzewski, Mike. *Leading With The Heart.* New York: Warner Books, 2000.

Lee, Albert. "Coach K Molded raw talent into greatness." University Wire, February 26, 1998.

Moran, Malcolm. "Krzyzewski's non-move proves moving; rejecting Lakers endears Duke coach to sport." *USA Today*, July 9, 2004.

The Official Website of the Basketball Hall of Fame. "Coach K Highlights." http://www.hoophall.com.

The Official Web Site of Coach Mike Krzyzewski. "Coach K and the Duke Community." http://www.coachk.com.

Sports Illustrated.com. "Krzyzewskiville: where the Cameron crazies live." http://www.sportsillustrated.cnn.com, February 26, 1998.

SportsStats. "Mike Krzyzewski Biography." http://www.sportsstats.com.

Young, Jim. "Duke beats Lakers: Coach K remains the big man on campus." *The News & Record* (Piedmont Triad, North Carolina), July 6, 2004.

Lord prepare me
to be a sanctuary